INTERNATIONAL BANKSTER$:

The Global Banking Elite Exposed and the Case for Restructuring Capitalism

THE UNDERGROUND KNOWLEDGE SERIES

James & Lance MORCAN

INTERNATIONAL BANKSTER$: The Global Banking Elite
Exposed and the Case for Restructuring Capitalism
Published by:
Sterling Gate Books
28 St. Heliers Place,
Papamoa 3118,
Bay of Plenty,
New Zealand
sterlinggatebooks@gmail.com

Special Note: This title is an extended version of Chapter 4 of *The
Orphan Conspiracies: 29 Conspiracy Theories from The Orphan
Trilogy* (Sterling Gate Books, 2014) by James Morcan & Lance
Morcan. This title therefore contains a combination of new material as
well as recycled material (in many cases verbatim excerpts) from *The
Orphan Conspiracies*.

Publication data:
Morcan, James 1978-
Morcan, Lance 1948-
Title: INTERNATIONAL BANKSTER$: The Global Banking Elite
Exposed and the Case for Restructuring Capitalism
Edition: First ed.
Format: Paperback
Publisher: Sterling Gate Books

Table of Contents

Introduction

Since the Global Financial Crisis of 2007-2008, many people around the world have been questioning whether there are certain figures or groups manipulating financial markets behind the scenes.

This speculation intensified with the ensuing government bailouts of privately owned banking institutions *ahead of* the millions of citizens facing bankruptcy.

As a result, many in the West now regularly second-guess their governments and assess any "financial relief packages" or "economic stimulus plans" with a high degree of suspicion and cynicism.

What certain corrupt politicians and so-called business leaders may have overlooked is that the public are not stupid, and what the average person lacks in specific knowledge of financial markets they make up for in spades with street smarts and life experience. That and the masses have finally caught on to what has been going on for decades, if not centuries, with the money men of the world.

There's a growing awareness in the general population of large-scale financial corruption by the global elite, or *the 1%*, if you will.

Surveys have also shown that a big percentage of the public feel they're being manipulated by corporations, banks, international interests and the media as well as by politicians who appear to have less respect for voters than ever before.

1

It's almost as if the public sense there must exist within government little-known powerbrokers who are not *for the people*, but actually against them. Powerbrokers who are essentially thieves operating in the shadows and getting richer and richer at the expense of the average citizen.

Let's face it, it's a really perverse world where we have almost unlimited military expenditure to finance wars, where our governments readily bail out privately-owned banks with multi-trillion dollar relief packages, and yet politicians tell us there is not enough money to cover the measly costs of our own citizens' basic healthcare, food, education and shelter.

Above: *An Occupy Wall Street protest against banks foreclosing homes.*
"Occupy Wall Street March 2012 foreclosure banner" by Mike Fleshman
Occupy Wall Street March 16, 2012, Uploaded by Gobonobo.
Licensed under CC BY-SA 2.0 via Wikimedia Commons

As to the question of who is responsible for this gigantic financial inequity, the prime suspects are the banking elite who are clearly some of the most powerful and influential people on the planet. They shape the modern world far more than politicians do in our opinion. After all, money can buy administrations. Some would even argue money can buy elections as well.

As a result of the public waking up to these sophisticated undercurrents beneath the surface of almost every major financial fraud, bankers are now held in about as high regard as criminal defence lawyers, used-car salesmen, debt collectors, arms traders and even drug traffickers.

We trust all this justifies our usage of the word *bankster* to describe throughout this book the morally questionable banking profession. *Bankster*, by the way, is a portmanteau or blend word derived from combining "banker" and "gangster". Its plural form, "banksters," refers to the commonly acknowledged predatory element operating within the financial sector.

We should point out, however, that whenever we use the term *bankster* it always denotes a high-level banker holding a senior position in the likes of major Wall Street banks, the Vatican Bank, the US Federal Reserve or the World Bank. So rest assured, the bank manager at your local branch is not (usually) a "bankster" and is unlikely to have been associated with any of the explosive financial crimes mentioned in this book.

This book is divided into two sections. Part One outlines the problems we've identified in banking and finance, while Part Two proposes possible solutions.

The first section is necessary because in order to consider solutions the problems must first be identified and dissected. Many books in this "exposing corruptions" genre offer no solutions to the problems; we hope you will agree that *INTERNATIONAL BANKSTER$* is not one of those.

In Part One, titled *The Financial Overlords*, we cover many of the major financial issues the world is enduring right now. Subjects include: the secret world of "black money" and the elite banking dynasties; the central banking system and the true nature of the US Federal Reserve; the less-than-holy financial activities of the Vatican Bank; the IMF and World Bank's sometimes less-than-charitable dealings with the Third World; the austerity measures currently being inflicted on vulnerable nations like Greece; as well as the theory that the world's money supply is essentially being created out of thin air.

In Part Two, titled *Potential Solutions*, we propose ideas for creating a fairer economic system. These ideas include: publicly owned banks; utilizing certain aspects of Islamic banking which may be compatible with Western banking systems; exploring whether capitalism *and* socialism can actually work in tandem; arguing the case to maintain but restructure capitalism; and predicting how cybermoney, or cryptocurrencies, will influence the world economy in the next few years.

We view the subjects covered in this book as being monetary issues on the surface only. In reality, they are humanitarian issues.

Starving the masses of financial opportunities, sinking them in debt and cheating them out of various services their taxes should pay for, are among the greatest sins those in power can commit. These sins result in widespread poverty, unemployment, increased crime rates, homelessness, drug addiction, overcrowded prisons and a whole host of other social problems.

We hope this book will contribute to the growing awareness in the mass populace that there is, contrary to what the Establishment tells us, enough wealth in the world to fix most of the biggest challenges our planet is currently facing.

James Morcan & Lance Morcan

Part One:
The Financial Overlords

1

Banksters On the Rampage

"What is robbing a bank compared to founding one?" –Bertolt Brecht, *The Threepenny Opera*

Y ou don't need to be a financial wizard to know that corruption is alive and well inside the global finance sector.

On a daily basis we are bombarded with mainstream news headlines confirming exactly that – the corruption rumors swirling about the European Union (EU) and the escalating Greek financial crisis being a case in point. (Escalating, that is, on the eve of the publication of this book). More about the Greek debacle later in this chapter.

Banks and bankers, of course, are at the very apex of the finance sector. So let's take a closer look at banking in the 21st Century.

Surprisingly, some of the most perceptive insights into today's banking system and the problems that pervade it are to be found within alternative media. It turns out there's a number of former bankers and money men (and women) to be found within the ranks of the *citizen journos*, or lay journalists, who 'man' these alternative media sites.

One of the best summaries of corruption of the banking system, in our opinion, is to be found on the appropriately named *TheAlternativeMedia.com* site. On that site, one Mitchell Cagle writes:

"Banks for decades have been the central source of where we save, manage and deposit our money. Many people do not know what actually goes on when your money is deposited. The bank uses your money to invest then gives you a fraction of what they make in interest. Sometimes that interest can actually end up being nothing due to the "fees" they actually charge that are excessive and fraudulent in most cases.

"Lately, banks have increased these fees some 54% resulting in profits of 34 billion dollars per year. It becomes increasing(ly) difficult to balance a checkbook anymore because of these "hidden fees". If you have a savings account, you are also being ripped off with monthly fees just for having the privilege".

Cagle lists the following as "examples of how we are being 'feed' to death by the banks:

"Banks engage in abusive practices that maximize overdraft fee revenue. The most common triggers of these fees are small debit card transactions that could easily be denied for NO fee.

"They charge exorbitant fees that bear NO relationship to the cost of covering an overdraft.

"They charge excessive numbers of overdraft fees over the course of a day, month or year.

"Automatically enrol customers in the most expensive overdraft protection possible.

"Monthly fees from nine dollars to thirty dollars for checking and savings accounts that used to be FREE.

"They push customers to use debit cards because it

cost them LESS to process but GOUGE retailers and customers because of the monopoly setup of the payment system".

But of course hidden fees are minor tools, or strategies, compared to other tricks of the trade employed by banksters.

A sea of never-ending debt

For a more 'qualified' insight into the money system, money markets and banking, you can't go past Ellen Brown's bestseller *Web of Debt*. An attorney, Ms Brown is founder of America's Public Banking Institute. She's also a harsh critic of what she describes as the money system.

Web of Debt's blurb reads:

"Our money system is not what we have been led to believe. The creation of money has been "privatized," or taken over by private money lenders. Thomas Jefferson called them 'bold and bankrupt adventurers just pretending to have money.' Except for coins, *all* of our money is now created as loans advanced by private banking institutions — including the *privately-owned* Federal Reserve. Banks create the principal but not the interest to service their loans. To find the interest, new loans must continually be taken out, expanding the money supply, inflating prices — and robbing you of the value of your money.

"Not only is virtually the entire money supply created privately by banks, but a mere handful of very big banks is responsible for a massive investment scheme known as 'derivatives,' which now tallies in at hundreds of *trillions* of dollars. The banking system has been contrived so that these big banks always get bailed out by the taxpayers from their risky ventures, but the scheme has reached its mathematical limits. There isn't enough money in the entire global economy to bail out the banks from a massive derivatives default today".

Even if Ms Brown is only partially right in that assessment, it still means there is a massive monetary predicament looming.

"The bankers and financiers are badly overplaying their hands, again, and people are starting to catch on to the scam. Real wealth is tangible things produced with tangible effort. Loans made out of thin-air 'money' require no effort and are entirely ephemeral. But if those loans are used to acquire real ownership of real assets, then something has been exchanged for nothing and one party is getting screwed." –Chris Martenson

Fiat Money

Many veterans of the banking and financial sectors have either stated or heavily implied that the world's money supply is essentially being created out of thin air and has no real value.

Those who subscribe to this school of thought say the shaky foundations of financial systems in the 21st Century is mainly down to the fact that all countries use *Fiat Money*, or inconvertible paper money made legal tender by government decree.

Throughout history, at various times and as recently as only several decades ago, other monetary systems were traditionally used such as *Commodity Money* or *Representative Money*. This meant the value of the money was either in the currency itself (e.g. real gold and real silver coins) or else the currency was a direct representative of a real commodity in physical storage (e.g. gold and silver certificates).

10

However, other financial whistleblowers argue the monetary and inflationary problems undermining the world at present have more to do with the fraudulent activities within elite banking circles than they do with the Fiat Money system.

Above: *What value do currencies really have?*
"Exchange Money Conversion to Foreign Currency"
by epSos.de –
Licensed under CC BY 2.0 via Wikimedia Commons

Banks slapped over proverbial wrist

This headline in *The Washington Post* edition of May 20, 2015, caught our eye: "Five big banks agree to pay more than $5 billion to settle regulatory charges." That sounded like a reasonably large fine to us…until one critic described it as "a slap on the wrist". When you consider the monies involved, that critic is probably right.

Excerpts from *The Washington Post* article follow:

"Five of the world's largest banks have agreed to pay more than $5 billion in fines to settle charges made by

11

regulatory agencies and the Justice Department that the banks had acted in concert to manipulate international interest and foreign currency exchange rates.

"Attorney General Loretta E. Lynch said the banks had engaged in 'brazenly illegal behavior ... on a near-daily basis.' She added that the deal showed that the government 'intends to vigorously prosecute all those who tilt the economic system in their favor (and) who subvert our marketplaces'."

The article continues, "The scale of the price-fixing scandal is hard to grasp, yet it touched, imperceptibly, almost every company and individual in the financial markets. By tweaking global benchmarks used to set foreign exchange and interest rates for a staggering number of transactions a day, the banks — over several years — bilked billions of dollars of extra profits by altering rates in their favor.

"Critics complained that the Justice Department had failed to prosecute any additional individuals... The fines, however, are among the largest ever. Barclays will pay $2.4 billion and fire eight employees who violated New York banking law for attempting to manipulate spot foreign exchange markets, in which $500 billion worth of dollars and euros are traded every day — five times as much as on all U.S. stock markets combined...

"Dennis Kelleher, president of Better Markets, a non-profit group, said that the Justice Department had not done enough, saying 'it talks tough, but winks at Wall Street's too-big-to-fail banks' criminal conduct, structuring sweetheart deals to minimize the impact on the criminals.' Kelleher said the fines alone wouldn't deter future criminal acts and that the Justice Department should punish bank executives and their supervisors for bad behavior. 'Banks don't commit crimes, bankers do,' he said".

"Banking is changing, slowly, but its culture is still corrupt." That's according to a headline in *The Guardian* newspaper's edition of November 16, 2014.

In the article beneath that revealing headline, *Guardian* columnist Will Hutton says, "Another week, another financial scandal. Six global banks, including RBS and HSBC, were fined £2.6bn last week for rigging the foreign exchange markets. Since 2008, total fines levied in Europe and the US for banking crimes and misdemeanours now top £100bn, with banks making provision for a further £60bn. British banks alone have set aside an estimated £30bn for fines, provisions and litigation costs."

Hutton asks, "What has gone wrong with Western finance?"

We are asking the same question.

Hutton continues, "The systemic ripping off of customers continued after the financial crisis to constitute what is now the biggest-ever global corporate scandal. Banks worldwide duped clients into buying products that were either not needed or provided no purpose. Worse, they organised financial markets whose purpose was to serve their own interests rather than those they purported to serve. It has proved a hard habit to break.

"British banks selling payment protection insurance (PPI) products on an industrial scale were doing what a street vendor in a bazaar might try. It shouldn't have happened but it's a perennial temptation. Finance is more exposed to this sort of risk, because customers are more credulous about financial products; and also because regulators have allowed banks to book the profits from products they sell on the moment of sale rather than over

13

their life".

Hutton concludes, "And yet reading the chatroom banter, with its echoes of the banter over mis-selling PPI, rigging interest rates or derivatives, offers a window into a very degraded culture. Making money from money, with the clients' interest last, is too dominant an element in the culture of investment bankers. Companies are seen by too many people, notably shareholders, as just instruments for self-enrichment".

But honestly, what can we expect from banksters when all they usually receive is a "slap on the wrist" from lawmakers whenever they get caught doing wrong?

"We know now that Government by organized money is just as dangerous as Government by organized mob." – Franklin D. Roosevelt

Wall Street shenanigans

In an article dated November 23, 2014 in *USA Today*, columnist John Maxfield predicts "There will come a time in the not-too-distant future when Wall Street banks won't be regularly chastised for ripping off customers, defrauding the federal and state governments, facilitating tax evasion, laundering money for sworn enemies of the United States, and manipulating bond, interest rate, foreign-exchange, and energy markets. When this time comes, however, it shouldn't be interpreted as a sign that things have changed".

Maxfield says, "Between 2012 and 2013, eight banks – UBS, The Royal Bank of Scotland, Rabobank, Deutsche Bank, Societe Generale, Barclays, JPMorgan Chase, and Citigroup – paid $6 billion to settle allegations that they manipulated the London interbank offered rate benchmark, one of the most widely tracked interest rate indexes in the world".

Among the examples he lists, from 2013, is a combined US\$9.3 billion payment from "more than a dozen banks... to make amends for systematically submitting fraudulent documents to courts in foreclosure proceedings".

Maxfield says, "Thus, the question is whether these practices are indeed isolated incidences of employee misconduct, as the banks would like us to believe, or instead whether they're indicative of a pattern of behavior that's endemic on Wall Street. I suspect it's the latter".

He concludes, "Of course, it's impossible to forensically prove that corruption is woven into the fabric of Wall Street banks – and, specifically, at companies with significant trading operations where the temptation to skirt the rules seems to be greatest. That's certainly what history suggests. And it's also what the ongoing regulatory assault on the industry implies. But, again, there is no way to quantitatively demonstrate this.

"But what we can say is that there is a noxious air of impropriety that has enveloped these operations. And, rightly or wrongly, this reputational baggage subjects shareholders of these banks to more risk than, at least in my opinion, is warranted by any reasonable estimate of future returns".

As Maxfield implies, the major Wall Street banks seem to have fraudulent activities down to a science and it's often virtually impossible to detect the sleight of hand in their activities.

"If a graduating MBA student were to ask me, 'How do I get rich in a hurry?' I would not respond with quotations from Ben Franklin or Horatio Alger, but would instead hold my nose with one hand and point with the other

toward Wall Street." –Warren Buffett

A Greek tragedy

Nowhere is the influence of the banks and the power of the international banksters better illustrated at present than in European Union (EU), especially as Greece's economic crisis deepens.

To better understand this latest Greek tragedy, it's helpful to understand the history behind it. One of the better summaries is to be found on the online site *CounterPunch.org* where, under the heading 'The view from Mount Olympus' (July 6, 2015), columnist Quincy Saul observes, "It seems that all the problems and solutions of the 21st century devolve today upon the people of Greece." He asks, "Have the people who invented democracy been reduced to a choice between poverty and austerity? Or can the current crisis be an opportunity to reclaim lost visions and values?"

Interviewing one Mikhalis Styllas, an educator, alpinist, geologist and activist, Saul asks his guest to explain the history behind the crisis. Styllas, who reportedly lives on Mount Olympus, explains that after 500 years of continuous strife "Greece was literally a wreck" when it emerged from the Greek Civil War (1946-49).

Styllas continues, "The wounds took many decades to heal (if they ever will) and…democracy was finally established in Greece following the collapse of a USA-planted dictatorship (1967 – 1974 junta), bringing a halt to many centuries of social and economic instability.

"As the country was trying to find its balance among "big ally" military and economic corporations…the standard of living gradually rose and a middle class was created".

Styllas says growth in the following decades "was fueled by uncontrolled borrowing from public and private banks" and from "an influx" of foreign funds.

He continues, "Poor political control over EU grants, combined with nearly a million public servants, plus corruption, tax avoidance and the fact that Greek society largely chose consumption instead of saving and investment, caused public debt to skyrocket".

Explaining Greece's relationship with the European Union, he says, "The EU has been partitioned between the northern (richer and financially more stable) countries and the southern (poorer) countries. When Greece entered the Eurozone and obtained the "Euro" as the new currency, things changed overnight...

"Access to easy money, publicized by Greek banks and local media, encouraged increasingly more Greeks to live beyond their means. Real estate was booming. People were buying new houses without taking into account signals from abroad, warning of a future blow-up".

In an article dated July 6, 2015, on the respected *GlobalResearch.ca* site, former US diplomat William R. Polk confirms that after the military junta was overthrown in Greece in 1974 corruption was rife.

Polk, who is a veteran foreign policy consultant, says, "The very rich used their money to create for themselves a virtual state within the state. They extended their power into every niche of the economy and so arranged the banking system that it became essentially extra-territorialized. Piraeus harbor was filled with mega-yachts owned by people who paid no taxes and London was partly owned by people who fattened off the Greek economy. The "smart money" of Greece was stashed abroad.

"This state of affairs might have lasted many more years, but when Greece joined the European Union in 1981, European (mainly German) bankers saw an opportunity: they flocked into Greece to offer loans. Even those Greeks who had insufficient income to justify loans grabbed them. Then, the lenders began to demand repayment. Shocked, businesses began to cut back. Unemployment increased. Opportunities vanished".

Polk continues, "There is really no chance that the loans will be repaid. They should never have been offered and never should have been accepted...

"Faced with German and EU demands for more austerity, the Greeks are angry. They have deep memories of hatred against the Germans (this time, not soldiers but bankers). They have been, time after time, traduced by their own politicians...And the bail-out package offered by the International Monetary Fund and the European Central Bank is heavily weighted against Greece".

Polk concludes, "Greeks also see their option of exiting the Euro as similar to stances taken by Britain and Sweden in not joining in the first place – although a painful adjustment for the Greek economy would be expected if Greece undertakes an unprecedented departure from the European currency".

At the time of this book's publication, news outlets are reporting that Greece leaving the Euro is a major discussion topic in the looming Greek national election.

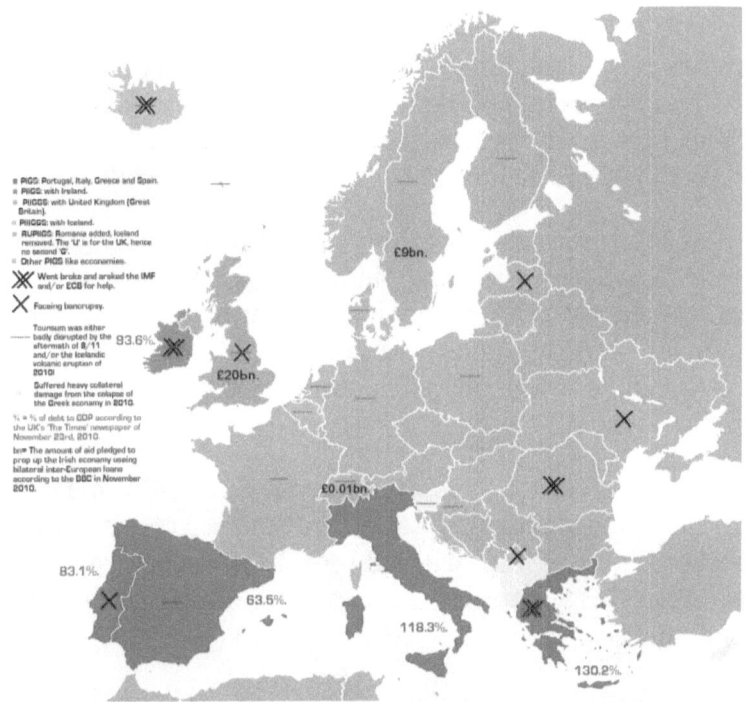

Above: *EU financial map with Greece & other nations in the red.*
"RUPIIGSmap"
The original author was Commons user Amibreton (talk)
the PIGS map derived from it was done
by Commons user Rannpháirtí anaithnid (talk).
Transferred from en.wikipedia to Commons
by Sfan00_IMG using CommonsHelper.
Licensed under CC BY-SA 3.0 via Wikimedia Commons

The FIFA kerfuffle

Banks, or their reputation at least, didn't fare too
well, either, in the latest corruption scandal surrounding
FIFA (the Fédération Internationale de Football
Association). A *Reuters* report in the June 22, 2015 edition
of the *Sydney Morning Herald* leaves no doubt the banks
could have done more to prevent the corruption.

The report states, "A global group of government anti-money laundering agencies said that financial institutions have not done enough to police suspicious financial activity by officials at soccer's global governing body FIFA, and cautioned banks to step up scrutiny.

"The warning from the Paris-based Financial Action Task Force (FATF) came in the wake of last month's indictment by the US of nine current and former FIFA officials and five business executives on a series of corruption charges, including bribery, money laundering and wire fraud".

The *Reuters* report continues, "With the US investigation continuing to widen, and a separate Swiss probe...the warning will add to banks' concern about handling certain soccer accounts for organizations and individuals...

"One question being asked in US banking circles is whether banks are acting quickly enough to flag activity once they have had subpoenas for information about an account from the authorities, said one source close to the industry...

"The acting US Attorney for the Eastern District of New York, Kelly T. Currie, told a news conference when the indictments were announced on May 27 that bank actions would be reviewed to see if they knowingly facilitated bribes. The banks concerned have not been accused of wrongdoing".

While the banks may not have been accused of wrongdoing, that's not to say they've done no wrong in the FIFA debacle.

The above *Reuters* report concludes, "The involvement of anti-money laundering monitors in current investigations of FIFA corruption was highlighted last week by Michael Lauber, attorney general of Switzerland.

"Lauber, who announced his FIFA investigation on the same day that US authorities revealed the indictments, told a news conference in Berne last week that his investigators were examining sets of suspicious transactions related to FIFA.

"He said that these transactions included 104 banking relationships, some of which involved multiple accounts, as well as 53 suspicious transactions which had been flagged by Swiss financial institutions to Switzerland's anti-money laundering agency".

Archbishop damns banking sector

There's nothing new about questioning the morality of banks and bankers, of course. In a *Daily Mail* article dated June 29, 2012, one George Carey, former Archbishop of Canterbury, delivered a damning critique of the banking sector – a sector he describes as "an important part of the network of institutions which build a civil society".

Former Archbishop Carey writes, "Thus evidence of corruption in our banks, and the resulting collapse of public trust in them, affects our very democracy.

"It is not an exaggeration to say that the sort of widespread alienation we are now witnessing among the public towards these multi-billion-pound behemoths can lead to civil unrest.

"Why? Because in more and more cases, naked greed seems to have been the driving force for many self-serving individuals in these institutions.

"That said, the real crisis we are facing is not a

financial but a moral one. And it is a direct result of the something-for-nothing culture which is poisoning our society".

Carey continues, "It seems utterly wrong that, at a time when banks have been rescued by the public purse to the tune of billions of pounds, they continue to dole out huge bonuses to their executives.

"To add insult to injury, they stand accused of refusing to lend to home-buyers and small businesses, thus causing even greater frustration and hardship for the hard-pressed man and woman in the street.

"Are they contrite? Hardly. All we see are greedy traders at Barclays systematically rigging interest rates to make their fortunes. And this comes just days after computer glitches at Nat West which left thousands of customers in uncertainty and financial trouble.

"It is hard not to conclude that institutionalised corruption is rife throughout today's banking industry…What is needed now is a determination to open up the banking industry to a proper public inquiry".

Archbishop Carey concludes, "Criminal charges must be brought where there is serious malpractice and corruption. This would only be a start, but at least it would begin to restore the public's faith in institutions which seem far more interested in profits than morals".

Above: *The Gold entrance to a Wall Street bank.*
"48-wall-street2"
by Phillip Capper from Wellington, New Zealand
Bank of New York Building entrance,
Wall St., Manhattan, Feb. 2008.
Licensed under CC BY 2.0 via Wikimedia Commons

Latest bank fraud cases

There appears to be another even bigger wave of bank fraud reports in the news media of late.

For example, on July 13, 2015, *Business Insider Australia* announced that "Hundreds of businesses are trying to figure out whether UK banks defrauded them via

LIBOR manipulation". LIBOR, incidentally, is the London Interbank Offered Rate, described by Columnist Lianna Brinded as a measure of the average interest rates banks are willing to lend to each other at.

Brinded writes, "Britain's biggest banks may have thought they had put the scandal involving misleading sales of complex interest rate derivatives to rest after they paid out over £2.4 billion ($US3.7 billion) in compensation to small business.

"But the LIBOR interest rate scandal – a seemingly separate issue – may have the potential to undo those settlements, sources tell Business Insider, if it can be shown that banks' manipulation of interest rates affected the derivatives they sold to small businesses.

Brinded continues, "The derivatives in question are financial products that were sold as "insurance" to businesses who wanted to be protected against high interest rates prior to 2008. However, the products were not insurance policies. They were interest rate swaps, a type of derivative deal that usually only occurs between investment banks or other large, sophisticated financial entities...

"When interest rates dropped after the 2008 financial crisis, hitting historic lows, businesses found themselves on the wrong side of their swaps deals and ended up paying the banks thousands of pounds a month in interest... Many businesses fell into financial hardship and some even went bankrupt...To date, 17,000 businesses — from family run shops to owners of a chain of hotels and care homes — have received redress".

Brinded concludes, "From 2012 to date, £1.9 billion ($US2.9 billion) has been paid in redress. This payout number is already considered small by politicians and lobby groups because many businesses have either lost their companies, downsized to the extent where they have even lost their family homes or had to axe staff to make ends meet. This number does not include private lawsuits that were made by businesses through the courts".

"Bankers own the earth. Take it away from them, but leave them the power to create money and control credit, and with a flick of a pen they will create enough to buy it back."
–Sir Josiah Stamp, former President, Bank of England

So how did the world get into such a financial bind?

There probably is no single answer to that question, and the truth likely involves various factors. Certainly, economists cannot agree with each other, that's for sure.

In the following chapters we will attempt to unravel the mystery by investigating elite banking families and the hidden system of finance (aka *Black Money*) as well as the history of modern banking...

2

The World's Hidden System of Finance

"There exists a shadowy government with its own Air Force, its own Navy, its own fundraising mechanism, and the ability to pursue its own ideas of national interest, free from all checks and balances, and free from the law itself." –Daniel K. Inouye, US Senator from Hawaii, in his testimony at the 1987 Iran-Contra Hearings.

It has been estimated by many an independent researcher that the bulk of the world's money supply is in the hands of less than 1000 families.

Yes, you read that right: *the bulk of the world's money supply is in the hands of less than 1000 families.*

These families include the likes of the Rockefellers, the Rothschilds, the British Royals as well as other elite dynasties. Their fortunes are said to consist of a mixture of Old World money, modern (declared) income, as well as *invisible* money and *blood* money.

In a similar vein, David Rothkopf's 2008 book, *Superclass: The Global Power Elite and the World They Are Making,* states that the world is governed by a group of 6000 elite individuals.

And according to Oxfam's 2014 economic briefing, the wealth of the top 1% in the world amounts to US$110 trillion. That's 65 times the total wealth of the bottom half of the world's population.

Another staggering statistic from Oxfam's briefing was that, collectively, the financial worth of the world's 85 wealthiest people approximately equals that of the poorer half of the world's total population. In other words, and *get this* – the richest 85 individuals have as much wealth as the 3.5 billion or so people who make up 50% of the world's population and who are categorized as the poorest on the planet!

What if those 85 *Rich Listers* got together – assuming they or their representatives haven't already – and agreed on certain financial things?

Things like bailing out private banks facing bankruptcy, lobbying for the amalgamation of various currencies, forcing austerity measures upon vulnerable nations sinking in debt or anything else that fits their definition of *a better world*?

With their financial clout and inherent power, surely almost anything imaginable would be achievable for the global elite. After all, who would have the power to stop this uber-powerful niche – the .000000001% of the world's population, who control the bulk of the world's money supply?

"Whoever controls the volume of money in any country is absolute master of all industry and commerce. And when you realize that the entire system is very easily controlled, one way or another by a few powerful men at the top, you will not have to be told how periods of inflation and depression originate." –James A. Garfield, 20th President

of the United States and one of only four presidents to have been assassinated.

Black Money

Beyond the official summaries of the world's wealth, and how few control it, there is in our opinion a hidden system of finance, which, if one day proven, will show there is an even greater gap between the global elite and the rest.

It's generally accepted the world's so-called 'Rich Lists,' from *Forbes* and the like, are not accurate in that their estimates of the *Rich Listers'* wealth are just that – estimates. However, according to our research, the world's wealthiest individuals don't necessarily even make the lists.

It has been purported by financial researchers and others in the know that there are individuals whose net worth would dwarf whoever tops the *Forbes Rich List* at any given time – net worth the likes of Bill Gates, Warren Buffett or Carlos Slim Helu could only dream about.

This may be hard to fathom, but it's important to consider two points when analyzing the finances of the global elite.

Firstly, without being able to inspect the bank accounts of billionaires, Forbes and similar Rich List publishers can only make crude *guesstimates* of individuals' true worth. As a result, their lists are anything but official and their accuracy is questionable – something the billionaire community is quick to point out.

Secondly, beyond those individuals and sums mentioned on the Rich Lists, there exists what is often referred to as *invisible* or *hidden wealth*. This involves non-disclosed fortunes that are virtually impossible to detect.

The planet's invisible wealth is comprised of undeclared income stashed away in offshore tax havens and Swiss bank accounts, secret *Old World* money and black market economies in which criminal enterprises conduct their business.

The criminal enterprises referred to include illegal drugs and arms dealing. One such arms dealer is Saudi Arabian Adnan Khashoggi who some banking and financial commentators estimate had a massive personal fortune of between US$2 trillion and US$7 trillion in the 1980's.

However, the world is still waiting for its first *official* trillionaire, and Khashoggi's fortune was only ever estimated by Forbes and the likes to be worth between $400 million and several billion. If the rumors of Khashoggi's multi-trillion dollar personal fortune were true then there's an extremely wide gulf separating unofficial and official estimates of his wealth.

The 2005 feature film *Lord of War*, directed by Andrew Niccol and starring Nicolas Cage and Ethan Hawke, is said to have been inspired by Russian arms dealer Viktor Bout. Like Khashoggi, Bout is rumored to have amassed a huge personal fortune impossible to estimate. Cage's character, a Ukranian-American arms dealer, is shown in the movie to be above the law with apparently unlimited money and resources.

The now deceased former Philippine President Ferdinand Marcos is another individual strongly rumored to have profited from the black market. Many who investigated Marcos, including politicians in the current Philippine government, say much of his wealth was secured from discoveries of the WW2 Japanese treasure hoard known as Yamashita's Gold. As the existence of those treasures was never acknowledged by any government, it's conceivable President Marcos could have amassed a large fortune impossible to trace or estimate. Some investigators say his secret bank accounts amounted to *trillions* of dollars.

If this sounds totally unbelievable, consider the television interview his widowed wife Imelda Marcos gave in 2009 for the *BBC TV* travel series *Explore*. While being filmed inside her lavish home in the Philippines, Imelda told *BBC* presenter Simon Reeve that her late husband was heavily associated with gold mining companies and also traded in gold. The former First Lady then presented Reeve with an official document. Although she would not allow the document itself to be filmed, Reeve confirmed it was a Certificate of Deposit made by Ferdinand E. Marcos in a bank in Brussels, Belgium, for the amount of *Nine Hundred and Eighty Seven Billion United States Dollars*. For those who don't have a good math brain, that's only 13 billion short of a trillion bucks.

If true, this sum in Marcos' Belgium bank account alone would be almost 13 times more than Bill Gates' total current fortune. The legacy of the former president becomes even more staggering when considering that this was just one of his bank accounts; the Philippine government has confirmed through investigations of its own that Marcos had many such secret accounts in banks all over the world.

Sticking with the theory that there are individuals worth far more than the names topping official rich lists, some say the Queen Elizabeth II is one of the wealthiest people, if not the wealthiest, in the world.

Above: *Queen Elizabeth II – what is she actually worth?*
"Elizabeth II" by Ricardo Stuckert/PR - Agência Brasil [1].
Licensed under CC BY 3.0 br via Wikimedia Commons

The majority of the Queen's wealth is said to be inherited money. After all, the British Royals descend from elite European families in a centuries-old empire that reaped the spoils of Ancient Rome, the Crusades and splits in the Vatican.

We are talking *serious* Old World money here. The Queen's ancestors not only owned untold mineral resources throughout the known world, but were also instrumental in setting up the earliest banks and controlling money supplies and lending. And the British House of Saxe-Coburg and Gotha – since renamed the House of Windsor – actively supported and profited from nefarious but extremely lucrative historical events like the opium trade in China as well as slave-trading.

Certain researchers suggest gold alone in the Royal Family's possession is said to be worth well over a trillion British pounds sterling.

And lastly, the world of Black Money is also said to be dominated by centuries old banking dynasties.

"For more than a century ideological extremists at either end of the political spectrum have seized upon well-publicized incidents such as my encounter with Castro to attack the Rockefeller family for the inordinate influence they claim we wield over American political and economic institutions. Some even believe we are part of a secret cabal working against the best interests of the United States, characterizing my family and me as internationalists and of conspiring with others around the world to build a more integrated global political and economic structure—one world, if you will. If that's the charge, I stand guilty, and I am proud of it." –David Rockefeller from his 2002 autobiography *Memoirs*.

Elite banking families

In a book on "international banksters," in a section on "financial overlords," we'd be remiss not to at least mention in passing the elite families who have been juggernauts in the history of global banking.

Families such as German financial dynasty the Oppenheim family who began to dominate the finance and banking sectors in Europe from the 18th Century onwards. One of the Oppenheim family's key assets for centuries, *Sal. Oppenheim*, was the highest valued privately owned investment bank in Europe until the family sold it in 2009.

An even more powerful banking clan is the almost infinitely-wealthy Rothschild family who also entered the banking industry in 18th Century Europe and used to own mining giant Rio Tinto.

Some say the Rothschilds have incalculable wealth and that even the price of gold is determined by them.

Above: *Elite 18th Century banker Baron Amschel Mayer von Rothschild.*
"Amschel Mayer Rothschild"
Licensed under Public Domain via Wikimedia Commons

In the United States, the Rockefellers are essentially the equivalent of the Rothschilds, or almost. Besides their extensive background in the oil business, the Rockefellers have long been an elite banking family with key investments like Chase Manhattan Bank and JP Morgan Chase.

Although it's not commonly reported or even investigated by mainstream media, it seems logical that these elite banking families would manipulate financial markets in their favor. Especially given they have dominated banking for centuries and have the process down to a fine art.

Another important point is these families made much of their fortunes through either criminal or highly immoral enterprises – perhaps deserving their "bankster" titles bestowed upon them by certain independent researchers.

For example, a June 26, 2009 article in the UK's *Financial Times* mentions the Rothschilds' and other elite banking families' historical links to slavery.

"Two of the biggest names in the City of London," the article states, "had previously undisclosed links to slavery in the British colonies, documents seen by the Financial Times have revealed.

"Nathan Mayer Rothschild, the banking family's 19th-century patriarch, and James William Freshfield, founder of Freshfields, the top City law firm, benefited financially from slavery, records from the National Archives show, even though both have often been portrayed as opponents of slavery".

The Rockefeller-associated asset, JP Morgan, is also listed in the *Financial Times* article as having ties to the slave trade.

"JPMorgan, the investment bank, set up a $5m scholarship fund for black students studying in Louisiana after apologising in 2005 for the company's historic links to slavery.

"In the case of Mr Rothschild, the documents reveal for the first time that he made personal gains by using slaves as collateral in banking dealings with a slave owner".

The article also names Lehman Brothers and the Bank of America as among other major financial institutions that profited off slavery.

"All problems, depressions, wars, disasters, assassinations – all of them were planned, caused, instigated, and implemented by the international bankers and their attempt to establish a central bank in every country in the world, which they have now done, thanks to corrupt politicians who have been bought and paid for. This is all you need to know about the history of the world." –Mary Elizabeth Croft

Could it be that some, or even many, of the world's recent financial problems – including meltdowns and crashes – are partly due to market manipulation these elite banksters (partially listed in this chapter) are doing in secret?

If the answer to that question is yes, then it is highly likely much of this subtle, semi-hidden manipulation of the "free market" is done via the much denigrated *central banks*.

3

The Central Banking System

"Under the guise of being nice guys, the central bankers have done to the people what no army in history has been evil enough to do." –Jarod Kintz, *This Book is Not FOR SALE*

A lot of the financial corruption exposed in this book relates – either directly or indirectly – to the central banking system.

But what is a central bank?

A central bank is a financial organization responsible for overseeing the monetary system of a nation. It manages a country's currency, sets interest rates and steers an economy toward inflation targets.

Central banks are also often called reserve banks. For example, the *Federal Reserve* (also known informally as *the Fed*) is the central banking system of the United States.

Other examples of central banks around the world include the People's Bank of China, the Reserve Bank of Australia, the Central Bank of Brazil, the Bank of Japan, the European Central Bank (ECB) and the Bank of England.

Elements of modern central banking systems have existed for around a thousand years and date back to The Song Dynasty (960-1279 AD) in China where the first circulation of a paper currency occurred.

The legendary Knights Templar – the wealthy Christian military order that reigned in medieval Europe for almost two centuries (1119-1312 AD) – ran a banking system that economists widely believe inspired present-day central banks, including the Federal Reserve in the US.

However, it wasn't until the 17th Century that the first official central banks were formed as certain nations such as the Netherlands, Sweden and the UK began to move away from commodity money (usually silver or gold) to circulating notes that simply represented 'promises to pay'.

From there, the central banking system spread like wildfire all around the world. Eventually, such banks cropped up everywhere from Africa and Central America to South America and Asia.

Above: *European Central Bank (ECB) building in Frankfurt.*
"ECB Frankfurt with Skyline" by Maslmaslmasl - Own work.
Licensed under CC BY-SA 4.0 via Wikimedia Commons

"In fact this is precisely the logic on which the Bank of England—the first successful modern central bank—was originally founded. In 1694, a consortium of English bankers made a loan of £1,200,000 to the king. In return they received a royal monopoly on the issuance of banknotes. What this meant in practice was they had the right to advance IOUs for a portion of the money the king now owed them to any inhabitant of the kingdom willing to borrow from them, or willing to deposit their own money in the bank—in effect, to circulate or "monetize" the newly created royal debt. This was a great deal for the bankers (they got to charge the king 8 percent annual interest for the original loan and simultaneously charge interest on the same money to the clients who borrowed it) , but it only worked as long as the original loan remained outstanding. To this day, this loan has never been paid back. It cannot be. If it ever were, the entire monetary system of Great Britain would cease to exist." —David Graeber, *Debt: The First 5,000 Years*

There are certain independent researchers, perhaps of the sensationalist variety, who have said "central banks are pure evil" or made other such alarmist statements. However, in reality, if a nation's central bank is managed *without internal corruption and without interference from foreign countries*, it should actually be a stabilizing force. In theory, a central bank can shield an economy from volatility in financial markets not to mention prevent fraudulent activities committed by commercial banks.

But the operative word, of course, is *corruption*. Throw corruption into the mix and central banks start veering toward the "pure evil" term some ascribe to them.

4

A short history of central banking in the US

"To live a more authentic life, I've started studying the world's best counterfeiters, the Central Bankers. But I can assure you, my love for you is not inflated." –Jarod Kintz, *This Book is Not FOR SALE*

Numerous economists and historians, and vociferous politicians like Senator Ron Paul and Governor Jesse Ventura, have opined that the global elite had been aiming to control the resources of the United States for centuries. Creating an American central bank privately owned by an international banking cartel seemed to be the most efficient way to achieve this aim.

In 1791, *the First Bank of the United States* was set up apparently because the Government had a massive debt left over from the Revolutionary War known as the American Revolution. Many researchers say this was the earliest attempt by banking families of the global elite to create a *privately-owned* US central bank, masquerading as a federally-owned entity.

Although the bank had numerous opponents in the political arena, it only controlled 20% of the nation's money supply – unlike the Fed today which manages 100% of the nation's money supply and not a 'penny' less.

American Founding Father and the nation's third President, Thomas Jefferson, was one of the most vocal critics of the First Bank of the United States. He argued the bank was unconstitutional, citing the 10th Amendment.

Jefferson also hinted that a central bank would lead to a monopoly instead of a free market. He said, "The existing banks will, without a doubt, enter into arrangements for lending their agency, and the more favorable, as there will be a competition among them for it; whereas the bill delivers us up bound to the national bank, who are free to refuse all arrangement, but on their own terms, and the public not free, on such refusal, to employ any other bank."

This experiment in US banking ended in 1811 when the bank's charter expired. Because of the institution's many critics, Congress decided not to renew its charter.

Above: *Philadelphia's historical site of the first US central bank.*
"First Bank of the United States"
Licensed under Public Domain via Wikimedia Commons

Six years later, in 1817, *the Second Bank of the United States* was brought into being as major international banking families continued to push for an American central bank. This bank was also quite temporary with President Andrew Jackson ending its existence only 15 years later.

However, the global elite's bankers did not give up, and in the early 20th Century started formulating ideas to create the US Federal Reserve System as we know it. One of the group's breakthrough ideas came during a secretive meeting at a hunting lodge on Jekyll Island, off the coast of Georgia, when they decided not to call the new bank a central bank. History had shown America did not want a central bank.

After much brainstorming, the deceptive *Federal Reserve* name was agreed upon – presumably because it was assumed this name would fool the public into thinking it was a government-owned bank.

Although representatives of this shadowy banking cartel were open to co-managing this new central bank with Congress, all agreed the bank's members had to be *private banks that would own all of its stock.*

"The accepted version of history is that the Federal Reserve was created to stabilize our economy. One of the most widely-used textbooks on this subject says: "It sprang from the panic of 1907, with its alarming epidemic of bank failures: the country was fed up once and for all with the anarchy of unstable private banking." Even the most naive student must sense a grave contradiction between this cherished view and the System's actual performance. Since its inception, it has presided over the crashes of 1921 and 1929; the Great Depression of '29 to '39; recessions in '53, '57, '69, '75, and '81; a stock market "Black Monday" in '87; and a 1000% inflation which has destroyed 90% of the

dollar's purchasing power." –G. Edward Griffin, *The Creature from Jekyll Island*

Above: *Seal of the 1913-established US central banking system.*
"US-FederalReserveSystem-Seal" by U.S. Government
Extracted from PDF version of the Federal Reserve's Purposes
& Functions document (direct PDF URL [1])
Licensed under Public Domain via Wikimedia Commons

(In book two of our international thriller series of novels *The Orphan Trilogy*, one of the founding members of an uber-powerful, shadowy organization is a senior banker of the US Federal Reserve, aka *the Fed*. It's a work of fiction, of course, but much of the research we did for that series has carried over to this book and to this chapter in particular).

If one day proven to be correct, the alternative theory surrounding the Federal Reserve is one that may explain a variety of unusual occurrences in financial markets over the years.

In a nutshell, this theory contends that the Fed is an institution that acts independent of the US Congress, has zero transparency or accountability, and even determines its own monetary policy.

5

Federal Reserve Act of 1913

"This [Federal Reserve Act] establishes the most gigantic trust on earth. When the President [Wilson} signs this bill, the invisible government of the monetary power will be legalized.... the worst legislative crime of the ages is perpetrated by this banking and currency bill." –Charles A. Lindbergh, Sr., 1913

In 1913, the banksters finally succeeded in creating a US central bank with the passing of the Federal Reserve Act. This bill, which had already been soundly defeated several times, appears to have come to fruition only because of well-orchestrated timing: the Federal Reserve Act was slipped through a skeleton Congress on December 23, 1913 when most of the bill's opponents had already left Congress for the holidays.

The Federal Reserve System, which was first devised in that secret meeting on Jekyll Island, was now codified by Congress and remains in effect to this day.

Fact: The Federal Reserve is the central bank of the United States even though it's not a part of the US Government.

Say what?

It's not a part of the government. Not even remotely.

But it says *Federal*! Surely it cannot be a privately owned organization?

The Fed is not a part of the government, *at all*.

Critics of the Federal Reserve say its sole purpose is to strip wealth from honest, hardworking American citizens and make the world's leading banking clans even richer.

Above: *The Fed's HQ in Washington D.C. (private property!).*
"Federal Reserve" by Dan Smith - Own work.
Licensed under CC BY-SA 2.5 via Wikimedia Commons

John Hylan, Mayor of New York City from 1917 until 1925, made some extraordinary statements in a speech he delivered in 1922. What Mayor Hylan said seems to confirm a grand conspiracy was indeed devised for the American banking system by the global elite.

"The real menace of our Republic is the invisible

government, which like a giant octopus sprawls its slimy legs over our cities, states and nation," said Mayor Hyland. "To depart from mere generalizations, let me say that at the head of this octopus are the Rockefeller-Standard Oil interests and a small group of powerful banking houses generally referred to as the international bankers. The little coterie of powerful international bankers virtually run the United States government for their own selfish purposes. They practically control both parties, write political platforms, make catspaws of party leaders, use the leading men of private organizations, and resort to every device to place in nomination for high public office only such candidates as will be amenable to the dictates of corrupt big business."

Only nine years after the Federal Reserve System was created, Mayor Hylan already seemed to be aware that this "invisible government" of "powerful international bankers" was controlling the US Government.

Cast your eye over these other quotes about the Fed and make up your own mind...

"The regional Federal Reserve banks are not government agencies...but are independent, privately owned and locally controlled corporations." –Lewis vs. United States, 680 F. 2d 1239 9th Circuit 1982

"Most Americans have no real understanding of the operation of the international money lenders. The accounts of the Federal Reserve System have never been audited. It operates outside the control of Congress and manipulates the credit of the United States." –Senator Barry Goldwater

"The Federal Reserve bank buys government bonds without one penny." –Congressman Wright Patman, Congressional Record, Sept 30, 1941

"The financial system has been turned over to the Federal Reserve Board. That Board administers the finance system by authority of a purely profiteering group. The system is Private, conducted for the sole purpose of obtaining the greatest possible profits from the use of other people's money." –Charles A. Lindbergh Sr., 1923

6

JFK vs. the Fed

"During the Kennedy Administration there was an unmistakable reconsideration of the relationship between the permanent wartime economy with the broader national and international political economy. This was evident not only in JFK's move to scale back US involvement in Vietnam, evident in National Security Action Memorandum 263, but also in his attempt to dismantle the Central Intelligence Agency, and challenge the power of the Federal Reserve Bank by issuing genuine silver-backed currency. In very short order such actions were overturned by Lyndon Johnson and the US was plunged into a murderous and costly war. With Kennedy's passing the world's inhabitants may have lost any serious prospect of world peace." –Prof. James F. Tracy, from article written for *Global Research*, November 25, 2012

Less than six months before he was assassinated, President Kennedy had begun formulating a new Federal Reserve Act, which many say would have restored the Fed to a fully-fledged US Government bank.

A little-known Presidential decree – *Executive Order 11110* – was signed by Kennedy on June 4, 1963. It would have deprived the Federal Reserve of its ability to loan money to the US Government at interest. By signing the document, President Kennedy was attempting to put an end to the Fed – or at least the Fed as we know it.

Without going into the specifics of Executive Order 11110, it arguably could have stopped the US from reaching its record-level national debt. As of the time of writing, the country's national debt is a crippling 17 trillion dollars – that's US$17,000,000,000,000 – and has increased at approximately 2 billion per day for the last 18 months.

Instead, JFK was assassinated as we all know. But what is less known is *the United States Notes* the President had issued as part of the executive order – notes which were designed to replace the Federal Reserve Notes – were immediately taken out of circulation.

Above: *A $5 United States Note due to Executive Order 11110.*
"US $5 1963 USN".
Licensed under Public Domain via Wikimedia Commons

"When Kennedy called for a return of America's currency to the gold standard, and the dismantling of the Federal Reserve System -- he actually minted non-debt money that does not bear the mark of the Federal Reserve; when he dared to actually exercise the leadership authority granted to him by the U.S. Constitution ... Kennedy prepared his own death warrant. It was time for him to go." –Colonel James Gritz, *Called to Serve: Profiles in Conspiracy from John F. Kennedy to George Bush*

49

To this very day, the Federal Reserve Notes remain in circulation as the currency all Americans use.

And, of course, what also remained post JFK was a central bank only nominally under the Government's control.

Above: *JFK tried to make the US banking system fairer.*
"John F. Kennedy, White House photo portrait, looking up"
by White House Press Office (WHPO)
Licensed under Public Domain via Wikimedia Commons

"Kennedy's fate was sealed in June 1963 when he authorized the issuance of more than $4 billion in United States Notes by his Treasury Department in an attempt to circumvent the high interest rate usury of the private Federal Reserve international banker crowd. The wife of Lee Harvey Oswald, who was conveniently gunned down by Jack Ruby before Ruby himself was shot, told author A. J. Weberman in 1994, "The answer to the Kennedy

assassination is with the Federal Reserve Bank. Don't underestimate that. It's wrong to blame it on Angleton and the CIA per se only. This is only one finger on the same hand. The people who supply the money are above the CIA". " –Jim Marrs, *Crossfire: the Plot that Killed Kennedy*

7

The Fed in the 21st Century

"Von Pein understood the entire monetary system was a gigantic Ponzi scheme and could be tampered with accordingly. He and his Federal Reserve cronies controlled interest rates, inflation and the printing of paper money. Thanks to him, funds from the Fed could be consistently funnelled into the Omega Agency via a multitude of offshore bank accounts." –The Orphan Factory

It has been estimated by independent researchers that eight banking families, including the Rockefeller family, own 75% to 85% of the shares in the Federal Reserve Bank. Many of the individuals in those families are also politicians. They include Republicans and Democrats, so clearly political allegiances make no difference. That's no surprise as it's almost common knowledge that the same financiers bankroll the campaigns of the two dominant parties in American politics.

Interestingly, most of the shareholders of the Fed are also members of the Bilderberg Group and/or the Council on Foreign Relations, which many independent researchers claim are elitist organizations.

After more than a century of these banksters having their way with little opposition, there has in recent times been a groundswell of resistance against the Fed. This resistance began as a grassroots movement early in the 21st Century and has really caught on in the last few years.

Two of the main reasons for the Federal Reserve conspiracy theory reaching popular consciousness were Ron Paul's presidential campaigns and the *Occupy* movement, that protest movement against economic and social inequality.

Congressman Ron Paul, a long-time critic of the Fed, said the following at the Republican GOP debate in Dearborn, Michigan, on October 9, 2007:

"What's happening is, there's transfer of wealth from the poor and the middle class to the wealthy. This comes about because of the monetary system that we have. When you inflate a currency or destroy a currency, the middle class gets wiped out... which is created by the Federal Reserve system benefit. So the money gravitates to the banks and to Wall Street."

Above: *Ron Paul posing for a Congressional portrait.*
"Ron Paul, official Congressional photo portrait, 2007"
by United States Congress
Licensed under Public Domain via Wikimedia Commons

And even more to the point, in a *CNBC* debate with Faiz Shakir on March 20, 2008, Ron Paul was asked to explain why he believes the Federal Reserve should not exist. Paul answered as follows:

"First reason is, it's not authorized in the Constitution, it's an illegal institution. The second reason, it's an immoral institution, because we have delivered to a secretive body the privilege of creating money out of thin air; if you or I did it, we'd be called counterfeiters, so why have we legalized counterfeiting? But the economic reasons are overwhelming: the Federal Reserve is the creature that destroys value. This station talks about free market capitalism, and you can't have free market capitalism if you have a secret bank creating money and credit out of thin air. They become the central planners, they decide what interest rates should be, what the supply of money should be".

Only a few years later, the *Occupy Movement* became headline news around the world after a series of dramatic protests. To paraphrase, the international protest organization's mission statement is to rally against inequality in all forms, especially economic inequalities. The Occupy Movement also aims to make the spread of wealth more evenly distributed amongst all sectors of society.

2011's *Occupy Wall Street* struck a chord with the masses, and the movement's ideals spread like wildfire from there. Less than a month after the Wall Street occupation began in New York City, there were protests all across America, and even more impressively in 82 countries worldwide.

During Occupy Wall Street, *End the Fed* and *Audit the Fed* were popular slogans used by protestors, and the mainstream media reported on these. *We are the 99%* proved to be an even more popular Occupy slogan – so much so that it soon became a worldwide catchphrase used by charities, television advertisers and common citizens.

Above: *An "End the Fed" Occupy placard.*
"Occupy Portland November 2, end the fed"
by Another Believer - Own work.
Licensed under CC BY-SA 3.0 via Wikimedia Commons

Primarily off the back of the awareness gained from the Occupy Wall Street movement and Ron Paul's 2008 and 2012 presidential campaigns, campaigners' desire that the Federal Reserve System be audited sparked nationwide interest.

In 2012, a bill inspired by this movement was passed through the House of Representatives with overwhelming bipartisan support. Called 'Audit the Fed', the bill was introduced into the House by Ron Paul.

However, since then, Paul's son Rand Paul launched an initiative to pass the same bill into the Senate. This debate is still ongoing as of writing, but it does not look likely to become law. Although the bill has some support in the Senate, Rand Paul currently faces stiff opposition from the likes of recently instated Federal Reserve Chair Janet Yellen and President Obama, to name but two.

Interestingly, although the banner for the 'Audit the fed' bill has been passed to his son, Ron Paul continues to champion the cause. As recently as September 14, 2015, he indicated in an article for *Newsmax.com,* a site which calls itself "America's News Page," that while he remains hopeful the audit legislation will go through he knows it's a long shot.

Ron Paul writes: "The only positive step toward addressing our economic crisis that the Senate may take this year is finally holding a roll call vote on the Audit the Fed legislation. Even if the audit legislation lacks sufficient support to overcome an expected presidential veto, just having a Senate vote will be a major step forward.

"Passage of the Audit the Fed bill would finally allow the American people to know the full truth about the Fed's operations, including its deals with foreign central banks and Wall Street firms.

"Revealing the full truth about the Fed will likely increase the number of Americans demanding that Congress end the Fed's monetary monopoly. This suspicion is confirmed by the hysterical attacks on and outright lies about the audit legislation spread by the Fed and its apologists".

Ron Paul continues, "Every day, the American people see evidence that, despite the phony statistics and propaganda emanating from Washington, high unemployment and rising inflation plague the economy".

He concludes, "Unless the people demand an end to the warfare state, the welfare state, and fiat money, our economy will continue to deteriorate until we are faced with a major crisis. This crisis can only be avoided by rejecting the warfare state, the welfare state, and fiat money".

Why are leaders so scared of having an audit of a supposedly federal organization?

Perhaps it's because there has never been a true, comprehensive audit of the Federal Reserve since the *institution began in 1913...*

"We have in this country one of the most corrupt institutions the world has ever known. I refer to the Federal Reserve Board and the Federal reserve banks. The Federal Reserve Board, a Government board, has cheated the Government of the United States out of enough money to pay the national debt. The depredations and the iniquities of the Federal Reserve Board and the Federal reserve banks acting together have cost this country enough money to pay the national debt several times over. This evil institution has impoverished and ruined the people of the United States; has bankrupted itself, and has practically bankrupted our Government." –Congressman Louis T. McFadden. 10 June, 1932

For an unashamedly biased viewpoint on banksters in the United States allow us to refer you to *AmericanBankster.com* – a site which, according to its homepage, is "dedicated to exposing the dangers of fiat money and the Federal Reserve System".

AmericanBankster.com's introductory statement reads (in part):

"In short, inflation is theft. Inflation results in a transfer of wealth from your bank account to those printing or creating new money; primarily the banksters at the Federal Reserve. This means that each and every year, the money in your bank account loses value not because of the "market", but because of the actions of the Federal Reserve. Under the Federal Reserve the dollar has lost 96% of its purchasing power. It would take only 4 cents in 1913 to buy a 2009 dollar.

"Many of us have been conditioned to believe that this is just the way things work, that inflation just occurs over time. Yet prior to the creation of the Federal Reserve, the dollar gained value over time, which is what it should do! This would make savings a real asset to you instead of a liability".

Among the headlines on the site's homepage is one drawing attention to the US Government's enthusiasm for printing money. The writer warns, "If President Obama and the Congress don't show any signs of easing up on SPENDING, then the Federal Reserve will have to increase the amount of dollars it prints.

"If it keeps printing dollars at this rate, then very soon we will see the effects of inflation begin, followed by hyper-inflation.

"Prices will spiral up and out of control and most of the middle class will become poor and the already poor will suffer the most. The cost of milk and bread will be prohibitively high. Small farms will go out of business, driving prices even higher as competition is diminished".

While still potentially *alarmist*, it is worth noting that these theories and predictions expressed by *AmericanBankster.com* probably would have been categorized as *lunatic fringe* several decades ago, *extreme* a decade ago, and *not quite mainstream* today.

As more 'underground knowledge' on banking, high finance and the way the world actually works is released to the public, who is to say whether such theories may not become commonly accepted by economists and academics alike in the coming years and decades.

8

Looting The World's Poor

"This book is also about the purposeful bankrupting of nations around the world, the inherently corrupt monetary system and the scam of modern banking – all of which have obviously become major vices of our era. I believe that financial domination is one of the main methods used to enslave the people of this world." –Dr. Takaaki Musha, from the foreword to *The Orphan Conspiracies*

Another facet of the global banking sector, and one that is often overlooked, is the international aid banks.

These include the World Bank and the International Monetary Fund (IMF).

Officially these financial organizations aim to reduce corruption in the Third World and in Developing nations as part of their poverty alleviation mission.

For example, in a press release from the World Bank itself on December 19, 2013, World Bank President President Jim Yong Kim stated that corruption is "Public Enemy Number One" in Developing countries.

"We will never tolerate corruption," Kim goes on to say, "and I pledge to do all in our power to build upon our strong fight against it."

That's all well and good, but what happens if there are corrupt elements operating in the highest echelons of the World Bank or the IMF?

And which organization would have the nous or wherewithal to monitor corruption within such charitable "corruption-busting" institutions?

"Western governments tax their citizens to fund the World Bank, lend this money to corrupt Third World dictators who abscond with the funds, and then demand repayment which is extracted through taxation from poor Third World citizens, rather than from the government officials responsible for the embezzlement. It is in essence a global transfer of wealth from the poor to the rich. Taxpayers around the world are forced to subsidize the lavish lifestyles of Third World dictators and highly-paid World Bank bureaucrats who don't even pay income tax." –Ron Paul's statement at the World Bank Hearing, May 22, 2007

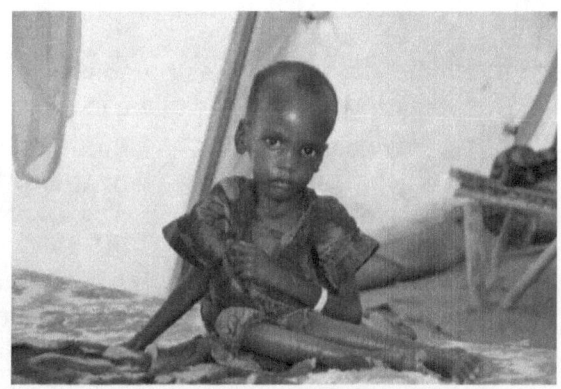

Above: *A starving child – Does the World Bank really care?*
"A malnourished child in an MSF treatment tent in Dolo Ado"
by DFID UK Department for International Development
Flickr: A malnourished child in an MSF
treatment tent in Dolo Ado.
Licensed under CC BY 2.0 via Wikimedia Commons –

A 2012 *Forbes* article headlined 'World Bank Spins Out Of Control' calls that organization "one of the world's most powerful institutions – charged with saving the world's poor – but also one of its most dysfunctional".

The article also refers to the World Bank as "an endlessly expanding virtual nation-state with supranational powers," and "little oversight by the governments that fund it".

The enlightening article goes on to say that "FORBES has also discovered a whole layer of bank officials who have learned how to game the system or expand their influence through its constantly revolving doors. It's not unlike the way that U.S. officials retire and then go to work for the contractors they associated with while in government service".

A 2013 article by Alex Newman, foreign correspondent for *The New American,* was even more critical of the World Bank and its lack of ability to stamp out corruption. It reads, in part, as follows:

"A former insider at the World Bank, ex-Senior Counsel Karen Hudes, says the global financial system is dominated by a small group of corrupt, power-hungry figures centered around the privately owned U.S. Federal Reserve.

"The network has seized control of the media to cover up its crimes, too, she explained. In an interview with *The New American*, Hudes said that when she tried to blow the whistle on multiple problems at the World Bank, she was fired for her efforts".

The article continues, "Hudes pointed out that a small group of entities — mostly financial institutions and especially central banks — exert a massive amount of influence over the international economy from behind the scenes. 'What is really going on is that the world's resources are being dominated by this group...At the heart of the network are 147 financial institutions and central banks — especially the Federal Reserve, which was created by Congress but is owned by essentially a cartel of private banks...This is a story about how the international financial system was secretly gamed, mostly by central banks — they're the ones we are talking about...The central bankers have been gaming the system. I would say that this is a power grab'."

Hudes is also quoted as saying the cartel of elite international banksters use the Fed and major private banks, in collaboration with other financial institutions such as The World Bank and the BIS (Bank for International Settlements), to complete shady financial deals, manipulate gold prices and conduct various other monetary deceptions.

"They got money for wars...But can't feed the poor." – Tupac Shakur

Confessions of an Economic Hit Man

One of the best testimonies toward the IMF and World Bank not always having honorable intentions toward the Third World is John Perkins' 2004 bestselling book *Confessions of an Economic Hit Man.*

The book describes how mysterious independent contractors known as economic hit men cheat poor countries all over the world out of trillions of dollars. They're paid large sums to creatively influence and/or bribe leading politicians in developing nations to make policy changes that suit multinational corporations. These policy changes usually revolve around either giving up the developing nation's resources to offshore interests or accepting large Halliburton-esque building contracts.

Perkins describes in *Confessions of an Economic Hit Man* how the main job of an economic hit man is to persuade the leaders of Third World nations to accept multi-billion dollar development loans from the IMF and World Bank.

Once economic hit men have carried out a *hit* on a nation, the profits automatically flow into the US while all the hard work is done by the impoverished citizens of the targeted nation.

Perkins claims he was formerly one of these economic hit men and was hired by America's National Security Agency (NSA) to carry out hits against vulnerable and mineral-rich Third World countries.

As Perkins writes in the book's preface: "Economic hit men (EHMs) are highly-paid professionals, who cheat countries around the globe out of trillions of dollars. They funnel money from the World Bank, the US Agency for International Development (USAID), and other foreign *aid* organizations into the coffers of huge corporations and the pockets of a few wealthy families who control the planet's natural resources. Their tools included fraudulent financial reports, rigged elections, payoffs, extortion, sex, and murder. They play a game as old as empire, but one that has taken on new and terrifying dimensions during this time of globalization. *I should know; I was an EHM*".

Above: *John Perkins, the (former) Economic Hit Man.*
"JohnPerkinsNov2009" by Justin Hoch.
Licensed under CC BY 2.0 via Wikimedia Commons

As a result of his tenure of many years as an EHM, of which he expresses much guilt, Perkins claims in the book that the developing nations he worked in were in the end crippled economically and virtually remote-controlled politically.

Perkins' confessions serve as an important reminder that the *winner takes all* mindset at the root of capitalism is a poison if left unchecked. That's not to say capitalism is bad per sē, or that a more refined version of it cannot work effectively. Nor does it mean the world should move toward socialism or communism, which have both proven throughout history to be just as disastrous. But surely the world's recent financial catastrophes and the bankrupting of individuals, families, small businesses, communities and entire nations, must make even the most ardent capitalist examine his or her beliefs.

9

Earthly Riches of the Vatican Bank

"A supplementary 180-page U.S. government report issued that spring (June 2, 1998) provided more evidence that neutral countries, including the Vatican, had profited by hiding Nazi gold in their central banks." –Gerald Posner, *God's Bankers: A History of Money and Power at the Vatican*

In our first non-fiction book *The Orphan Conspiracies: 29 Conspiracy Theories from The Orphan Trilogy*, we devote a chapter to mysterious deaths of various high profile individuals, including JFK, Princess Diana, Martin Luther King and Marilyn Monroe – and also a gentleman who will forever be remembered as the Smiling Pope.

Pope John Paul I, who was nicknamed *the Smiling Pope* due to his forever-cheerful demeanor, was elected the Catholic Pope on August 26, 1978. Just 33 days later, at 5am on September 28, John Paul I was found dead, marking the end of one of the shortest reigns in papal history.

Anomalies, discrepancies and conspiracy theories abound around the circumstances of John Paul I's death. The Vatican's official version of events leading up to the death changed at least once and the Pope's body was embalmed before an autopsy of the corpse could be done.

Possible conspirators include international banksters operating within the Vatican Bank, Freemasons and even the Vatican itself. In fact, that's the most common theory – that it was an *inside job*.

Despite his constant smile, Pope John Paul I was apparently hell-bent, so to speak, on reforming the Vatican, and many have argued the Catholic powers-that-be were simply protecting their position by assassinating him.

Above: *Pope John Paul I's tomb beneath the Vatican*
"Tomb of pope Johannes Paulus I"
by it:Utente:Riccardov - my photo.
Licensed under Public Domain via Wikimedia Commons

Top of the Smiling Pope's to-do list was said to have been fixing the large scale corruption he believed existed within the Vatican Bank. The same religious financial institution which only a few decades earlier had lucrative collaborations with Benito Mussolini's fascist regime and Adolf Hitler's Nazi Party, and had strayed into many other areas not generally associated with the Holy Spirit, was about to be brought into line.

According to this murder theory, Vatican banksters weren't too keen on being reformed. Nor did they resonate with the possibility of being forced to confess their sins, so they sent the Pope to an early grave.

In a case of circumstantial evidence, the President of the Vatican Bank in 1978 was American archbishop Paul Marcinkus who just happened to be seen walking briskly through the Vatican at dawn and around the exact time Pope John Paul I had died. That could obviously be a coincidence, but then again Marcinkus wasn't known for early morning walks.

Granted, conspiracy theorists also say the Pope was assassinated by non-money men in the Vatican for other planned radical reforms, including allowing for Catholics around the world to practice contraception. However, to our way of thinking, the theory connecting John Paul I's death to the Vatican banksters is pretty compelling.

The common consensus between researchers and even many Catholics is that there are more than enough dark factions operating within the Vatican to have carried out such a murder.

Which got us thinking…How wealthy is the Vatican Bank (officially known as the Institute for Religious Works or *Istituto per le Opere di Religione* in Italian) and, indeed, how wealthy is the Vatican itself? How did it, or does it, generate its wealth? And how does it use its wealth?

For answers to these and quite a few other questions, you can't do much better than read investigative journalist

Gerald Posner's bestselling book, *God's Bankers: A History of Money and Power at the Vatican*. Endorsed by *The New York Times* as "A deeply reported, fast-paced exposé of the money and the cardinals-turned-financiers at the heart of the Vatican—the world's biggest, most powerful religious institution," *God's Bankers* is described by more than a few reviewers as "a riveting read!"

The New York Times, incidentally, describes author Gerald Posner as an acclaimed journalist with "exhaustive research techniques." We'd have to agree.

The blurb for God's Bankers reads:

"From a master chronicler of legal and financial misconduct, a magnificent investigation nine years in the making, this book traces the political intrigue and inner workings of the Catholic Church. Decidedly not about faith, belief in God, or religious doctrine, this book is about the church's accumulation of wealth and its byzantine entanglements with financial markets across the world. Told through 200 years of prelates, bishops, cardinals, and the Popes who oversee it all, Gerald Posner uncovers an eyebrow-raising account of money and power in perhaps the most influential organization in the history of the world.

"*God's Bankers* has it all: a rare exposé and an astounding saga marked by poisoned business titans, murdered prosecutors, mysterious deaths of private investigators, and questionable suicides; a carnival of characters from Popes and cardinals, financiers and mobsters, kings and prime ministers; and a set of moral and political circumstances that clarify not only the church's aims and ambitions, but reflect the larger dilemmas of the world's more recent history. And Posner even looks to the future to surmise if Pope Francis can succeed where all his predecessors failed: to overcome the resistance to change in the Vatican's Machiavellian inner court and to rein in the excesses of its seemingly uncontrollable financial quagmire. Part thriller, part financial tell-all, this book shows with extraordinary precision how the Vatican has evolved from a foundation of faith to a corporation of extreme wealth and power".

Reviewers' comments reveal that readers resonate with *God's Bankers*. Two reviews in particular caught our eye.

This review (excerpt) from *Portsmouth Herald*:

"This fast-paced, carefully researched exposé of the nefarious enrichment of the Vatican is a real eyebrow-raiser....a spellbinding, intricate tale of corruption, intrigue, and criminality at the heart of the world's largest religious institution".

And this review from *Financial Advisor Magazine*:

"A book worth the time if a reader is interested in Roman Catholic Church and European history....The book will be appreciated by those involved in finance. It is chock full of tales of investment schemes involving off-shore ghost companies, shell corporations and holding companies set up to hide the movement of money, the use of tax havens, tax laws (and how to avoid them), and financial instruments that caused millions of dollars to disappear...Some may also appreciate reading about the personalities of popes, the power games and the internecine politics of the Roman Curia (the pope's administrative wing) that make the current political games played in Washington, D.C., seem amateurish by comparison".

Above: *St Peter's Square, Vatican City.*
"St Peter's Square, Vatican City - April 2007"
by Diliff - Own work.
Licensed under CC BY-SA 3.0 via Wikimedia Commons

"Like many, I feel the disconnect between the barefoot carpenter who preached on hillsides and the papal aristocracy; between the man who ate, slept, and taught in the desert and the man who takes his meals from fine china and silver in the majesty of the Vatican and controls billions of dollars' worth of real estate and banks." – William Friedkin, The Friedkin Connection: A Memoir

The British newspaper *The Telegraph* does a good job of summarising the history of the Vatican Bank and the problems that have plagued it in an article by columnist Jules Gray, dated September 5, 2014.

Gray writes, "Perhaps more than any other, the Vatican Bank should be expected to maintain the highest of moral standards in the way it conducts its business. However, despite its saintly links, the bank that acts on behalf of the Catholic Church has developed a reputation for corruption, scandal and mismanagement over the last

71

few decades.

"Murder, bribery, suspicious deaths, money laundering, and many other nefarious acts have been linked to the bank that is officially known as The Institute for Works of Religion (IOR)…".

Gray continues, "Like the Catholic Church, the Vatican Bank has been steeped in mystery for much of the time it has been in operation. Founded in 1942 as a means to manage money on behalf of the Catholic Church, its main purpose was to 'provide for the safekeeping and administration of movable and immovable property transferred or entrusted to it by physical or juridical persons and intended for works of religion or charity.' It was plunged into disrepute in the late 1970s after many years of rumours about money laundering on behalf of the mafia…

"While the scandals of 30 years ago are yet to be fully put to bed, new ones have emerged in recent years that have sent the Vatican Bank back into the murky spotlight of before. In 2009 the bank was being investigated by authorities over money-laundering worth €180m. More allegations followed against then IOR President Ettore Gotti Tedeschi… although charges were never brought".

Gray concludes, "Further allegations then emerged over money laundering – which led to US investment bank JP Morgan closing one of the Vatican Bank's accounts – after it failed to provide sufficient information about the sources of the €1.8bn deposits…Pope Francis established a new Pontifical Commission to study potential reforms for the bank, which later led to four senior cardinals being sacked".

A more recent article in the same newspaper, *The Telegraph*, provides eye-opening insights into the amount of cash that passes through the Vatican Bank's coffers. This particular article, penned by Rome correspondent Nick Squires and dated May 25, 2015, reads in part as follows:

"Once tainted by scandal and intrigue, the Vatican bank has managed to increase its profits by more than 20 times since embarking on a comprehensive drive for transparency and accountability ordered by Pope Francis.

"The bank announced on Monday that it earned €69.3 million (£49 million) in 2014 – up from €2.9 million the previous year".

Squires continues, "Profits plummeted in 2013 as a result of a dramatic dip in the value of the bank's gold reserves, two substantial write-offs and the cost of employing a team of forensic accountants to review the murkiest corners of its finances.

"The outside consultants were brought in to bring the bank…into compliance with tough anti-money laundering regulations.

"The gold price did not move in our favour (in 2013) and there were the extraordinary effects of two substantial write-offs, one on an investment equity fund made by the previous management of the bank and the other on a bond issue for a media company," Max Hohenberg, a bank spokesman, told *The Telegraph*.

"Plus we had high consultancy and legal fees to pay. So 2013 was not a normal year – we had a massive clean-up of the balance sheet. Now we are back to normal…".

Squires concludes, "Until the reforms ordered by Pope Francis, the bank had a distinctly patchy record on financial propriety and transparency."

Most notorious was the Vatican Bank's involvement in the bankruptcy of Italy's largest private bank, the Banco Ambrosiano, in 1982.

Its president, Roberto Calvi, nicknamed "God's Banker", was found hanged beneath London's Blackfriars Bridge, with investigators unable to rule whether he had committed suicide or was murdered, possibly by the Mafia.

Above: *God's Banker Roberto Calvi may have been murdered.*
"Roberto Calvi" by Unknown
Foto extraída de la revista Siete Días.
Año XV, numero 797, septiembre de 1982.
Licensed under Public Domain via Wikimedia Commons

In an article dated June 27, 2012, *Forbes* columnist *Avi Jorisch* provides a less flattering summary of the Vatican Bank's finances.

Jorisch, a former U.S. Treasury Department official, writes, "Italian prosecutors have now detained the former head of the Vatican's bank after searching his home and former office for suspected criminal behavior.

"Catholics and followers of the Holy See will be disappointed to learn that the Vatican's bank appears to be embroiled in yet another financial scandal. After a number of very embarrassing episodes in recent years, the Pope pledged to comply with international standards on illicit finance and clean up the bank's image. The European Union has an important role to play in helping the Vatican mitigate risk and come into full compliance; the Financial Action Task Force (FATF), set up by the G-7 to combat money laundering and terrorist financing, has a responsibility as well...".

Jorisch continues, "The bank accepts deposits only from top Church officials and entities, according to Italian legal scholar Settimio Caridi. It is run by a president but overseen by five cardinals who report directly to the Vatican and the Vatican's secretary of state. Because so little is known about the bank's daily operations and transactions, it has often been called "the most secret bank in the world...".

"Tedeschi and the Vatican Bank have recently been investigated on two separate occasions for money laundering. This past March, JP Morgan Chase closed a Vatican account in Milan after the IOR was "unable to respond" to questionable money transfers, according to Italy's leading financial newspaper, Il Sole 24 Ore...".

Jorisch concludes, "In today's interconnected financial world, instituting measures to mitigate abuse of the international financial sector is part of the cost of doing business. Unquestionably, one of the most serious public policy challenges the international community will face in the foreseeable future is how to use every tool in its arsenal to make progress against those who exploit tainted money. While the Vatican answers to a higher calling, the EU, FATF and MONEYVAL should insist that its earthly responsibilities are equally important".

Well said Mister Jorisch! It's all very well (the Vatican) answering to a higher calling when earthly responsibilities – not to mention laws and good citizenship – are by all accounts all too often ignored. At least not where money's concerned.

"The Institute of Applied Economic and Social Research at the University of Melbourne published the results of an extensive study of international money laundering. The authors compared the banking systems of two hundred countries. The Vatican ranked in the top ten money laundering havens, behind Luxembourg, Switzerland, the Cayman Islands, and Liechtenstein, but ahead of Singapore." –Gerald Posner, *God's Bankers: A History of Money and Power at the Vatican*

As for that leading question: How much is the Vatican worth? An exhausting search reveals that no-one really knows. Certainly no-one outside the Vatican – and they ain't saying.

Perhaps the Pentecostle Church site *Christian Assemblies International* sums it up best. It quotes the following excerpt (abridged) from Avro Manhattan's perceptive book *The Vatican Billions*:

"The Catholic Church...once all her assets have been

76

put together, is the most formidable stockbroker in the world. The 'Wall Street Journal' said that the Vatican's financial deals in the U.S. alone were so big that very often it sold or bought gold in lots of a million or more dollars at one time.

"Therefore, the Vatican was, and still is, the most redoubtable wealth accumulator and property owner in existence. No one knows for certain how much the Catholic Church was, or is worth in terms of dollars and other currencies, not even the pope himself.

"That is the true situation borne out by a Vatican official who, when asked to make a guess at the Vatican's wealth today, replied very tellingly, 'Only God knows'."

10

Banking Chicanery in Modern America

"America's been ruined by one word: Bankers. No, two words: Bankers and lawyers. Make that three words. Add politicians to that list. Oh, and don't forget the lobbyists."
–Jarod Kintz, *The Days of Yay are Here! Wake Me Up When They're Over.*

P artly because of the aforementioned issues surrounding the Federal Reserve System, and partly because of the enormous size of the United States economy, there are arguably more deceptions within banking in America than anywhere else in the world. And despite the media regularly highlighting banking fraud, and the constant promises from political leaders to place tough reforms on major banks, many financial investigators report corruption to be at an all-time high in the US banking sector.

Pundits still argue over how big a role corruption played in America's recent financial crisis. Most agree, however, the US needs to toughen bank reforms.

A *Financial Times* report, dated July 7, 2015, addresses this very issue. Columnist Barney Jopson reports, "The International Monetary Fund has called for the US to defend and strengthen its Dodd-Frank financial reforms, adding fuel to the intense debate over how to balance stability and growth on Wall Street.

"In its first comprehensive assessment of the American financial system in five years, the IMF said the US needed to toughen regulation to ward off a repeat of the last financial crisis".

Jopson continues, "The intervention comes as Republicans in Congress seek to water down Dodd-Frank because they say it stifles prosperity, while Democrats accuse the GOP of wanting to grant reckless favours to Wall Street.

"The IMF said: 'Before the memory of the crisis begins to fade, it will be important to complete the reform agenda and resist attempts to overturn previously agreed measures. It is, therefore, critical that rulemaking under the Dodd-Frank act should be completed and implementation of several other agreed measures should begin'."

Incidentally, the Dodd-Frank act is a Wall Street Reform and Consumer Protection Act designed to promote the financial stability of the United States by improving accountability and transparency in the financial system, to end "too big to fail", to protect the American taxpayer by ending bailouts, to protect consumers from abusive financial services practices, and for other purposes.

It was signed into federal law by President Barack Obama in July 2010.

However, as the *Financial Times* report suggests, the American public still need to wait to see if the Dodd-Frank act is fully implemented – or, if it is overturned or otherwise subjugated.

As of the time of writing this book there are ongoing Constitutional challenges to the act, which are before the Court of Appeals for the District of Columbia Circuit. The legal complaints, which cite Constitutional concerns, have asked the court to rescind the law, arguing it gives federal government too much unaccountable power.

Above: *President Obama – against fraud or a tool of banksters?*
"Official portrait of Barack Obama" by Pete Souza
The Obama-Biden Transition Project
Licensed under CC BY 3.0 via Wikimedia Commons

"It is well that the people of the nation do not understand our banking and monetary system, for if they did, I believe there would be a revolution before tomorrow morning." – Henry Ford

Wall Street bonuses

If the size of bonuses being paid out to US bankers isn't indicative of a corrupt banking system, we're not sure what is. While Americans employed on the minimum wage struggle to get by on little more than $7 per hour, we learn that in 2014, Wall Street banks paid out billions in bonuses to their employees.

While that may not be corrupt technically, in every other sense it surely is.

The media watchdog site *PRwatch.org* carries an interesting article by Sarah Anderson, of the Institute for Policy Studies, on this blatant inequity.

Dated March 12, 2015, the article reads:

"Wall Street banks handed out $28.5 billion in bonuses to their 167,800 employees last year, up 3 percent over 2013, according to new figures from the New York State Comptroller. These annual bonuses are an extra reward on top of base salaries in the securities industry, which averaged $190,970 in 2013. To put these figures in perspective, we've compared the Wall Street payout to low-wage workers' earnings. We've also calculated how much more of a national economic boost would be gained if similar sums were funneled into the pockets of the millions of workers on the bottom end of the pay scale".

Ms Anderson continues, "The $28.5 billion in bonuses doled out to Wall Street employees is double the annual pay for all 1,007,000 Americans who work full-time at the current federal minimum wage of $7.25 per hour. Wall Street bonuses rose 3 percent last year, despite a 4.5 percent decline in industry profits. The size of the bonus pool was 27% higher than in 2009, the last time Congress increased the minimum wage.

"Wall Street's bonus culture, we learned from the 2008 financial industry meltdown, creates an incentive for high-risk behaviors that endanger the entire economy. A large share of low-wage earners, on the other hand, spend

81

every workday meeting basic human needs, such as providing food services and taking care of the disabled and elderly…".

"While workers' wages stagnate, the Wall Street bonus culture is flourishing—in part because of regulatory foot-dragging".

Surely that summary can only be viewed as an indictment on the entire financial system and the politicians charged with protecting everyday workers?

"Myth: Feeding the banking sector gobs of welfare cash will bring about a recovery. Fact: Our leaders are only dedicated to preserving power." –Ziad K. Abdelnour, *Economic Warfare: Secrets of Wealth Creation in the Age of Welfare Politics*

The morality of governments rescuing banks

The US Government's bailout of *Big Business* – banks included – has long been a bone of contention. Supporters of the bailout policy, including many economists, insist something is needed to encourage confidence in American markets while opponents argue the policy does nothing more than incentivize risk-taking and reward poor decisions.

We'd go further than that and ask why banks and other firms should be kept afloat by the taxpayer when their reckless business decisions backfire?

Government bailouts are not unique to banks of course. It wasn't that long ago the Government stepped in to bailout America's flagging auto industry by way of a handsome rescue package for General Motors Corporation and Chrysler. That bailout, in 2008, was followed a year later by the bailout of Bank of America.

Nor are government bailouts the exclusive domain of America. According to *Wikipedia*, "World Bank reported (in 2000) that banking bailouts cost an average of 12.8% of GDP. The report stated: Governments and, thus ultimately taxpayers, have largely shouldered the direct costs of banking system collapses. These costs have been large: in our sample of 40 countries governments spent on average 12.8 percent of national GDP to clean up their financial systems".

The *EBSCOhostConnection* site provides a concise overview of recent bank bailouts in the US. It confirms public interest in the phenomenon has peaked "because of large and far reaching bank bailouts in the wake of the 2008-2009 economic crisis".

The article reads, in part, as follows: "The economic crisis that began in 2007 and took hold in 2008-2009 is believed to be a direct result of risky investments, reckless decision making, and investors taking on greater risk in the hopes of greater returns. The government's concern about the failure of banks is tied to the role banks play in the larger economy—as sources of credit or lenders to businesses. Banks also work on the demand side, by extending credit to customers...".

The report continues, "Many lenders found creative ways to give mortgages to buyers who might otherwise not qualify for a loan. As a result, the housing market grew and houses increased in price—some beyond their value.

"When the housing market collapsed and as prices plunged, interest rates on adjustable rate mortgages

(ARMs) increased and the economy began to weaken; thus, borrowers could not afford the loans they had been given, with many holding mortgages that exceeded the value of their homes. Foreclosures resulted, and many hedge funds, which specialized or had their basis in the resale of mortgage-backed securities, failed. Business sectors related to the housing market also felt the collapse, including construction, finance, and real estate...".

The *EBSCOhost* report concludes, "Debate over the efficacy and the execution of these bailouts continued into 2009, with some believing that government intervention is not the answer, and that it rewards poor decision making on the part of companies and mortgage borrowers. Others fear greater government control, possible mismanagement, and poor oversight. In spite of the criticism, economists and others argued that something needed to be done to ensure confidence in US markets, as well as prevent an economic crisis".

The bailout of Bank of America warrants special attention as it constitutes one of the biggest payouts of taxpayer monies in US history. A January 16, 2009 *Reuters* report of that sorry slice of history reads as follows:

"Bank of America Corp was rescued by the U.S. government on Friday through a $20 billion bailout and a guarantee for almost $100 billion of potential losses on toxic assets to cushion the blow from a deteriorating balance sheet at Merrill Lynch & Co, its recently acquired brokerage.

"The bailout makes Bank of America the biggest recipient of taxpayer money next to Citigroup as the government pours cash into the nation's banks to plug holes left by bad loans. The worst housing crisis since the Great

Depression and the worst recession in many years have hammered U.S. banks.

"The capital is on top of $25 billion that Bank of America previously got from the Treasury Department's Troubled Asset Relief Program (TARP) in October and is the latest indication that authorities are still struggling to come to grips with the financial crisis that began about 18 months ago...".

The report continues, "In return for the bailout, Bank of America, which just a few months ago was trumpeting the Merrill takeover as a coup, agreed to cut its dividend to 1 cent per share from 32 cents and cap executive pay -- concessions similar to those made by Citigroup when it was rescued in November...

"The guarantee also resembles the $306 billion backstop that Citigroup received...A U.S. official said President-elect Barack Obama's transition team had been notified of the Bank of America negotiations. Earlier, a financial policy source told Reuters that both President George W. Bush and Obama, who takes over on Tuesday, have signed off on the package of support".

The *Reuters* report concludes, "Bank of America sought the aid to absorb growing credit losses at Merrill, whose acquisition was completed on January 1, creating the largest U.S. bank".

Above: *Another private bank saved by taxpayers' money.*
"Bank highlander" by Brian Katt at English Wikipedia
Transferred from en.wikipedia to Commons.
Licensed under CC BY-SA 3.0 via Wikimedia Commons

Bankers, government economists and others (with vested interests) are quick to defend the bailouts policy, arguing that where marketplace confidence and business stability are at stake, such a policy is justified. In terms of logic, to the ears of these two laymen at least, their arguments sound reasonably convincing.

However, in terms of morality – keeping in mind Bank of America and others foreclosed on many home mortgages and small business loans during the economic crisis – the political decision to bailout private banks don't sit right with us. Those on the sharp end of the foreclosures were customers of the bank, and they didn't have anyone to bail them out.

We come back to our original question and ask why banks and other such firms should be kept afloat by the taxpayer when their reckless business decisions backfire?

If you come to the same answer we did, then surely the system (the system of banking and government) itself is corrupt.

Part Two:
Potential Solutions

11

Is There a Fairer Economic System?

"We have come a long way in our understanding of human motivation and of the blind operation of our economic system. Now we realize that dislocations in the market operation of our economy and the prevalence of discrimination thrust people into idleness and bind them in constant or frequent unemployment against their will. The poor are less often dismissed from our conscience today by being branded as inferior and incompetent. We also know that no matter how dynamically the economy develops and expands it does not eliminate all poverty." –Dr. Martin Luther King, Jr., *Where Do We Go From Here: Chaos or Community?*

Given at this point in time more and more countries are on the verge of economic collapse, more and more individuals are facing unemployment, bankruptcy and homelessness, and reports of the global elite not paying taxes and illegally stashing funds in offshore tax havens are ever-increasing, sooner or later the common people will demand a fairer economic system.

What form that economic system will take is anyone's guess.

It is very obvious to us social reforms are needed to balance the cruel inequities that exist in a world where the 99% aka the common people have very little say on financial matters whilst that tiny but nevertheless powerful minority we call *banksters* thrive and grow ever more influential. Even more cruel when you consider those in the latter category thrive in a financial climate that exists because of economic decisions made, and legislation passed, by politicians they've either directly or indirectly bankrolled.

A common theme that seems to be emerging in the mass populace is the idea that capitalism and the free market should be allowed to flourish, but only *after* the people have been cared for.

In other words, basic human rights such as food, shelter, education and healthcare should be provided to all citizens *first* out of a government's tax revenue. After those expenses have been taken care of, then *and only then* should the government step aside and allow the wonders of private enterprise and the free market to work their magic.

"I have always said that I am in favor of a minimum income for every person in the country." –F. A. Hayek, from *Hayek on Hayek: An Autobiographical Dialogue*

Universal income

Thinking further on this need to look after the common people *before* worrying about whether the free market is operating efficiently enough, one intriguing idea is to establish a 'universal income' for all citizens.

Such a scheme would work in the same way as universal healthcare, which provides healthcare (and financial protection) to *all* citizens irrespective of their financial status or annual income.

The very definition of *universal healthcare* signals that a nation's health and income go hand in hand, which leads to our next question...

Could a universal income actually benefit our society?

One city in the Netherlands seems to think so.

On June 26, 2015, one headline in UK newspaper *The Independent* read: "Dutch city of Utrecht to experiment with a universal, unconditional basic income." The article describes how University College Utrecht, a town within Utrecht, is running an experiment to see if society can prosper with a "universal, unconditional income" for all citizens.

Excerpts from *The Independent* article follow:

"Basic income is a universal, unconditional form of payment to individuals, which covers their living costs. The concept is to allow people to choose to work more flexible hours in a less regimented society, allowing more time for care, volunteering and study".

The reporter quotes a Utrecht spokesman as saying, "Our data shows that less than 1.5 percent abuse the welfare. But, before we get into all kinds of principled debate about whether we should or should not enter, we need to first examine if basic income even really works. What happens if someone gets a monthly amount without rules and controls? Will someone sitting passively at home or do people develop themselves and provide a meaningful contribution to our society?"

Utrecht is apparently looking to expand the experiment into other municipalities and is currently awaiting permission from The Hague to broaden the trial.

Above: *The city of Utrecht in the Netherlands.*
"Utrecht-Uithof, from CambridgeLaan 01".
Licensed under Public Domain via Wikimedia Commons

It turns out the Dutch are not the only ones to trial such a scheme.

In the mid-late 1970's, all the residents of Dauphin, in Manitoba, Canada, also received a basic welfare income. Amazingly, poverty was all but eliminated in Dauphin, and most of the city's residents and officials said it was a resounding success. However, when a more Right Wing government was voted into power at the end of that decade the experiment was immediately discontinued.

The Huffington Post is one of the few well-known

media outlets to have run an article on this little-known but groundbreaking Canadian social experiment. The headline for its article, published on December 23, 2014, says it all: *A Canadian City Once Eliminated Poverty And Nearly Everyone Forgot About It.*

The article reads, "Between 1974 and 1979, residents of a small Manitoba city were selected to be subjects in a project that ensured basic annual incomes for everyone. For five years, monthly cheques were delivered to the poorest residents of Dauphin, Man. – no strings attached".

The reporter states that "poverty was completely eliminated" for the five years the experiment ran.

The report continues, "The program was dubbed 'Mincome' – a neologism of 'minimum income' – and it was the first of its kind in North America. It stood out from similar American projects at the time because it didn't shut out seniors and the disabled from qualification.

"The project's original intent was to evaluate if giving cheques to the working poor, enough to top-up their incomes to a living wage, would kill people's motivation to work. It didn't".

When Canada's Conservative Government swept into power in the late 1970's, it not only scrapped the project and refused to implement the project in other Canadian cities, it also prevented a final report from being released on Mincome's impact on the residents of Dauphin.

Decades later, in 2011, a summary report of sorts was finally released in the form of a research paper. The paper specifically documented how Mincome affected people's health using census data. It turns out overall hospitalization rates (for accidents, injuries, and mental health diagnoses) dropped in the group whose members received basic income supplements.

To summarize, by *giving* the community's poorest residents sufficient income to comfortably survive there was a positive impact on Dauphin's healthcare system.

It could also be concluded from the research data that a guaranteed annual income policy could actually save governments millions or even billions of dollars in social welfare spending, especially for poverty-induced healthcare.

Given the success of Mincome, and the trial now underway in Utrecht, it's a mystery to us why the concept hasn't at least been trialed elsewhere in the world – especially as numerous economists and big thinkers have reportedly wondered aloud whether a universal income could work for the benefit of society.

One such thinker was American architect, systems theorist, author, designer, inventor R. Buckminster Fuller (1895-1983) who wrote the following:

"We should do away with the absolutely specious notion that everybody has to earn a living. It is a fact today that one in ten thousand of us can make a technological breakthrough capable of supporting all the rest. The youth of today are absolutely right in recognizing this nonsense of earning a living. We keep inventing jobs because of this false idea that everybody has to be employed at some kind of drudgery because, according to Malthusian Darwinian theory he must justify his right to exist. So we have inspectors of inspectors and people making instruments for inspectors to inspect inspectors. The true business of people should be to go back to school and think about whatever it was they were thinking about before somebody came along and told them they had to earn a living."

Above: *Buckminster Fuller proposed universal income.*
"BuckminsterFuller1"
by en:User:Edgy01 (Dan Lindsay) Own work.
Licensed under CC BY 3.0 via Wikimedia Commons

On the one hand, we are supportive of these theories as they seem to protect everybody from extreme poverty. On the other hand, we are concerned implementation of such ideologies might be too socialistic, causing some – or perhaps many – individuals to lose their motivation, their sense of ambition or their entrepreneurial spirit.

Then again, the 'basic wage' we have in mind wouldn't be so high that beneficiaries of the handout would become complacent or lazy. On the contrary, it would simply be the equivalent of a 'retainer,' or base salary, to keep people from going hungry, or becoming homeless or bankrupt, or falling ill because they can't afford healthcare.

We concede that a sector of society would abuse the privilege. It's obvious a percentage of recipients of a basic wage would fritter it away – be it on gambling, alcohol, drugs or other similar activities. Such collateral damage would need to be weighed against the benefits of a universal income.

Essentially, it would be a minimum income simply for *being human*, covering bare essentials such as food, education, shelter and medicine. If its use could somehow be restricted to cover bare essentials, or survival costs, then possibly this radical idea has great merit.

Hell, think of all the lives a universal income would save, not to mention all the crime it would reduce. To our way of thinking, from a humanitarian perspective at least, implementing such a system transcends other economic debates currently doing the rounds.

Although it could probably be classified a socialist measure, a universal income needn't interfere with the free market system. After all, we are only talking survival monies here, and the vast majority of people would still want to improve their lives and would be prepared to work hard to achieve that.

Not convinced? We'd remind you of the off-the-radar wealth that exists in the world right now – wealth that could be partly channeled to cover social expenditures such as those we've outlined. Wealth like that exists. We know that. It exists in offshore tax havens and in the secret world of *black money* and in the elite banking sectors.

Beyond the examples of massive, undeclared wealth already given, it's also worth mentioning another staggering example.

In 2012, Republican Alan Grayson questioned the

Federal Reserve Inspector General Elizabeth Coleman as to where $9,000,000,000,000 (nine trillion dollars) had gone missing.

Coleman admitted she hadn't a clue and also that her agency has "no jurisdiction to investigate, or audit" the Fed.

Incidentally, those missing monies would equate to $30,000 per US citizen.

And still politicians keep telling the voting public that social measures such as universal income or universal healthcare are unaffordable.

Go figure!

"The contemporary tendency in our society is to base our distribution on scarcity, which has vanished, and to compress our abundance into the overfed mouths of the middle and upper classes until they gag with superfluity. If democracy is to have breadth of meaning, it is necessary to adjust this inequity. It is not only moral, but it is also intelligent. We are wasting and degrading human life by clinging to archaic thinking. The curse of poverty has no justification in our age. It is socially as cruel and blind as the practice of cannibalism at the dawn of civilization, when men ate each other because they had not yet learned to take food from the soil or to consume the abundant animal life around them. The time has come for us to civilize ourselves by the total, direct and immediate abolition of poverty." – Dr. Martin Luther King, Jr., *Where Do We Go From Here: Chaos or Community?*

12

Islamic Banking

"Banking as it should be" –Abu Dhabi Islamic Bank slogan

One of the most aggressive aspects of the traditional banking system, for individuals and entire countries, is the crippling interest rates which banks charge and which compound year after year.

Perhaps Islam can provide the world with a fairer banking system.

Islamic banking, or banking that upholds the principles of Sharia (Islamic law), involves the prohibition of interest or fees for loans. Besides applying no interest over the term of loans, banking under Sharia principles means certain types of investments deemed sinful – investments in alcohol for example – are not allowed.

What's interesting is that although Sharia law has existed in the Middle East and Muslim communities for many centuries, it's only in the last 15 to 20 years that large Islamic banks have been formed to strictly carry out Sharia finance principles.

"It is very attractive to non-Muslims. As recently as yesterday, when I had dinner with one of my friends, I was telling him about how we conduct our business. He's Czech, and he said, 'I wish my bank was like that'." –Petr Klimeš, head of marketing, Abu Dhabi Islamic Bank

In *Heaven's Bankers*, author Harris Irfan describes the secret world of Islamic banking. The following excerpt from book's blurb highlights many of the positive benefits some economists say exist within Islamic finance:

"A trillion dollar financial industry is revolutionizing the global economy. Governments and corporations across the Islamic world are increasingly turning to finance that complies with Shari'a law in order to fund economic growth. Even in the West, Islamic finance is rapidly becoming an important alternative source of funding at a time when the conventional finance industry is reeling from the effects of the financial crisis.

"From its origins in the seventh century, Islamic finance has sought to develop core ethical principles that are based in the foundations of Islam and Shari'a. By engaging critically with the complexities of international finance, it has evolved and adapted into a world emerging from the economic and moral aftermath of a global financial crisis. But with an increasing Western interest, is it able to remain true to the principles of its faith? Can it maintain its ideals of social justice? Or is Islamic finance guilty of the very dangers it seeks to avoid?"

Other financial analysts, however, claim that Islamic banking is no real solution and is basically the same as Western banking except they don't use the word 'interest'.

One example we came across compares the terms of a

standard 30-year mortgage in a Western bank to those of an Islamic bank. To our surprise, the projected mortgage payments equated to roughly the same by term's end. Strange considering a big percentage of any mortgage is interest, and Islamic banks supposedly cannot legally charge interest. This possibly indicates that Islamic banks still make as much profit as their Western counterparts, and at the end of the day their customers are no better off.

Regardless, Islamic banking is spreading around the globe.

It's not only Muslim countries adopting, or considering adopting, banking based on Sharia law. For example, a 2012 article on the Czech Republic's *Radio Prague* website outlines a debate on the possibility of adopting some or all of Islamic banking's principles in the European Union.

An excerpt from this article follows:

"A good deal of the ongoing economic and financial turmoil on world markets has been blamed on the unscrupulous practices of the international banking and financial sector. Islamic banking, on the other hand, is seen as a fairer and more balanced alternative which has been much less affected by the crisis. Can the Czech Republic benefit from a financial system based on the Islamic law?

"Based on the principles of Islamic law, or Sharia, Islamic banks are prohibited from charging interest, speculating as well as investing in businesses considered unethical by Islamic scholars. Instead, Islamic or participant banking offers a system of shared risks and profits, and its supporters claim it is committed to promoting equity, moderation and social justice".

The *Radio Prague* article concludes, "Islamic

banking is today the fastest growing segment of the financial system, and is also considered a more honest and fairer alternative to conventional banking."

Above: *An Islamic bank in London, England.*
"Islamic Bank of Britain in Edgware Road
geograph.org.uk - 1041561" - by Basher Eyre.
Licensed under CC BY-SA 2.0 via Wikimedia Commons

"What's important for our non-Muslim costumers is what they will get at the end of the day. They might not necessarily be interested in whether the transaction is compliant with Sharia but they don't mind. They are interested in the value they get and they are very happy with it." –Petr Klimeš

We wonder whether the West could take the best of Islamic banking principles and introduce them into their own (banking) systems? Naturally, not everything from the

Islamic approach to finance can be adopted in the West, especially as Sharia law opposes some of the principles of Western or Christian societies.

It would take greater minds than ours to suggest exactly how this could work. However, in the interests of fairness, even we can see there may well be a case to adopt what works in the Islamic banking system and introduce it, or at least trial it, in the West.

13

Publicly Owned Banks

"It is more profitable than Goldman Sachs Group Inc., has a better credit rating than J.P. Morgan Chase & Co. and hasn't seen profit growth drop since 2003. Meet Bank of North Dakota, the U.S.'s lone state-owned bank, which has one branch, no automated teller machines and not a single investment banker." –The Wall Street Journal

It seems to us that all the fraudulent behavior in banking will never go away so long as we, 'the people,' are left on the sidelines and elite business interests, or banksters, remain in control.

We are all for private enterprise and allowing the free market to work unimpeded, but given the atrocious track record of banksters surely it's time for governments to reclaim some ownership in the banking sector.

One idea that seems ridiculously simplistic but may actually have merit, is creating public banks that can work *for* the people instead of *against* the people.

A public bank is a financial institution in which the state or government are the owners. In theory, it should mean less corruption as the main goal of any public asset is not to make profits, but to serve the country's population.

There are public banks operating now in various

countries, including France, Argentina, Germany, Italy, Brazil, Chile, Norway, Portugal, Russia and Spain.

There is even one such bank in the US – The Bank of North Dakota, which was established in 1919 to promote agriculture and industry in North Dakota. The bank is the only government-owned asset of its type in America.

Two books by Ellen Brown, an attorney and founder of America's Public Banking Institute, whom we quoted in Chapter 1, may provide some solutions...

Web of Debt is a book, which, according to its blurb, "unravels the deceptions in our money scheme and presents a crystal clear picture of the financial abyss towards which we are heading".

The blurb continues, "Then it explores a workable alternative, one that was tested in colonial America and is grounded in the best of American economic thought, including the writings of Benjamin Franklin, Thomas Jefferson and Abraham Lincoln. If you care about financial security, your own or the nation's, you should read this book".

Brown's latest book, *The Public Bank Solution*, is appropriately tag-lined "What Wall Street doesn't want you to know," and it promotes the public bank alternative.

In that book's blurb, the author writes, "Shock waves from one Wall Street scandal after another have completely disillusioned us with our banking system; yet we cannot do without banks.

"Nearly all money today is simply bank credit. Economies run on it, and it is created when banks make loans. The main flaw in the current model is that private profiteers have acquired control of the credit spigots. They can cut off the flow, direct it to their cronies, and manipulate it for personal gain at the expense of the producing economy.

"The benefits of bank credit can be maintained while eliminating these flaws, through a system of banks operated as public utilities, serving the public interest and returning their profits to the public. This book looks at the public bank alternative, and shows with examples from around the world and through history that it works admirably well, providing the key to sustained high performance for the economy and well-being for the people".

According to the Public Banking Institute, positive benefits of establishing public banks include the following:

-Make affordable loans to small businesses, farmers, government entities, and students

-Save taxpayers up to 50% on critical infrastructure like bridges and trains and schools

-Eliminate billions in bank fees and money management fees for cities and states

-Support a vibrant community banking sector

-Enable sustainable prosperity

Also, according to a November 2014 article in *The Wall Street Journal* by reporter Charles Dawson, the aforementioned publically-owned Bank of North Dakota has outperformed Wall Street in recent times.

Dawson writes, "Its total assets have more than doubled, to $6.9 billion last year from $2.8 billion in 2007. By contrast, assets of the much bigger Bank of America Corp. have grown much more slowly, to $2.1 trillion from $1.7 trillion in that period.

105

"Return on equity, a measure of profitability, is 18.56%, about 70% higher than those at Goldman Sachs and J.P. Morgan...

"Standard & Poor's Ratings Services last month reaffirmed its double-A-minus rating of the bank, whose deposits are guaranteed by the state of North Dakota. That is above the rating for both Goldman Sachs and J.P. Morgan and among U.S. financial institutions, second only to the Federal Home Loan Banks, rated double-A-plus".

In explaining the Bank of North Dakota's public banking model, Dawson continues, "It traditionally extends credit, or invests directly, in areas other lenders shun, such as rural housing loans ... Retail banking accounts for just 2%-3% of its business. The bank's focus is providing loans to students and extending credit to companies in North Dakota, often in partnership with smaller community banks ... The bank's mission is promoting economic development, not competing with private banks ... It recently started offering mortgages to individuals in the most underserved corners of the state".

Above: *An Occupy Wall Street protestor promotes public banking.*
"Day 21 Occupy Wall Street October 6 2011 Shankbone 3"
by David Shankbone - Own work.
Licensed under CC BY 3.0 via Wikimedia Commons

"The profession of banking has been overwhelmed by the short-term-focused, transaction-driven business of banking. In our search for solutions, we should be open to exploring deeper direct engagement by the public sector, with all proper caveats regarding governance and political influence. ... A careful state-by-state examination of public banking is an important part of the broad financial system transformation the Capital Institute seeks." –John Fullerton, Founder and President, the Capital Institute.

Given all the volatility and the long history of corruption in the private banking sector, the obvious question is: Why aren't there more public banks by now?

Surely governments around the world owe it to their citizens to at least explore public banking.

14

Capitalism *and* Socialism?

Capitalism and socialism are traditionally thought of as being contradictory and conflicting economic ideologies that cannot operate in tandem. However, that assumption has been challenged in recent years with some radical thinkers claiming to be equal parts socialist and capitalist – and, in some cases at least, presenting sound arguments for combining the two contrasting ideologies.

According to traditional definitions in economic theory, such statements are paradoxical. However, perhaps two systems that were formerly thought to be mutually exclusive, or diametrically opposed, may actually share some common ground.

British journalist, author and economics editor Paul Mason may well be one of the aforementioned radical thinkers. In an article published in *The Guardian* on July 17, 2015, Mason writes about "new ways of working and the sharing economy".

An excerpt from the article follows:

"The old ways will take a long while to disappear, but it's time to be utopian.

"Technology has created a new route out, which the remnants of the old left – and all other forces influenced by it – have either to embrace or die. Capitalism, it turns out, will not be abolished by forced-march techniques. It will be abolished by creating something more dynamic that exists, at first, almost unseen within the old system, but which will break through, reshaping the economy around new values and behaviours. I call this postcapitalism".

Private citizens are starting to think along these lines also – as these excerpts show from a September 2015 letter addressed to the editor of Californian-based daily newspaper the *Chico Enterprise-Record* from local resident Linda Furr:

"Capitalism, socialism can co-exist peacefully.

"There's socialism in Norway, yet there's capitalism, too. Norway's forms of capitalism and socialism check each other. People in Norway decided long ago they want to have a good, working economy as well as good investments in their country's future, i.e. education, health care, affordable transportation, freedom from want as much as possible, innovations in arts, science and engineering".

Ms Furr concludes, "Whatever the reason, Norway's forms of capitalism and socialism seem to be working well — certainly far better than the casino-styled, vulture capitalism of our country — in place still, in spite of the havoc it wreaked on the world in 2008".

We note other countries, like Japan for example, also seem to be successfully supporting big business as well as looking after their population by incorporating the best of capitalism *and* socialism.

"We put our faith in a system that awards do-nothing CEOs with millions as their companies collapse and

110

provoke a global crisis. We judge corporate success on the number of sackings, fund the privatisation of essential services with public money and favour cheap goods discounted by the loss of our jobs. We sign up for wars in which capitalism makes a killing." –Bob Ellis, *The Capitalism Delusion*

Above: *Cover for an economic book by Hans-Hermann Hoppe.*
"A Theory of Socialism and Capitalism 2010 edition cover"
Licensed under CC BY 3.0 via Wikimedia Commons

Polling the underground

In 2014, we founded a discussion group on *Goodreads.com*, the popular literary site for readers and authors. Called *Underground Knowledge*, the group was established to encourage dialogue about underreported issues of our time.

We recently ran a poll on the subject of capitalism, asking fellow 'Undergrounders' (group members) to vote on this question: *Do you believe capitalism should be restructured, replaced by another economic system or left exactly as is?*

During the voting period, a lively discussion unfolded in the comments below the poll's results. Some of these comments are included here. Before you read them, we must point out that the worldwide membership of the Underground Knowledge group is comprised of a diverse bunch of intelligent and revolutionary thinkers, and spans the political spectrum from the Left to the Right, or from Liberal to Conservative and virtually every political persuasion in between.

Fellow Undergrounders include bestselling authors, internationally-renowned scientists, investigative journalists, economists, social activists and whistleblowers, doctors, former intelligence agents, ex-military officers and even a former NASA engineer.

Anyway, on the subject of capitalism, here's their comments:

Member 1: "I'm essentially a Capitalist as I believe (however flawed) Capitalism is the only economic system ever devised that rewards entrepreneurial and/or hard-working individuals. So I'd never vote for Socialism or communism. However, I also think unregulated Capitalism has become one of the biggest problems facing society right now. It is allowing big business (including multinational monopoly-style companies) too much power and the average 9-5 worker is getting screwed. So I think there needs to be social reforms, but not Socialism, if that makes sense."

Member 2: "Communism need not be the only alternative to Capitalism. A system should be devised which incorporates the good from both."

Member 3: "The system worked post war to about 1998 fairly well. We have to stop income gaps and we need to tell the oligarchs to check how their greed worked out in France in 1789."

Member 4: "There is such abuse of capitalism. A tragic example is the negligence of controls on pipelines that constantly cause serious environmental disasters, as well as take lives. Oil drilling without proper controls as seen in the Gulf here with the continual leakage of oil barely covered by the media. The proposed, possibly disastrous, drilling in the Arctic is another example. When money is the only objective at any cost you have a problem. The proposed TPP trade agreement is inherently wrong, again giving more power to the corporations. If you look at the 1888 introduction to Edward Bellamy's Looking Backward you will see the workers still in the same position today. There must be social, economic, governmental and political change. Accountability must be instituted for corporations, none of which, including banks are too big to fail. War profiteering must end. Endless war must end. No one needs excessive billions of dollars at the expense of everyone else. Economic morality must be sadly legislated."

Member 5: "I believe, capitalism although it sets free for decision and ambition which is unfortunately the way this world we have set for us keeps turning, Capitalism also excludes the proletarian masses, the people who should have a voice as well, then we only hear the whispers of injustice. Capitalism should be reformed, so freedom can be secure for all, and finally the ones who were once left behind can be reached."

Member 6: "The greatest flaw of capitalism is the ability of corporate leaders to manipulate the political system to their benefit and to the detriment of everyone else. Making behavior like this a criminal offence, and enforcing the law, would go a long way toward reforming capitalism. To paraphrase Churchill, capitalism is the worst economic system there is, except for all the others."

Member 7: "I think that capitalism is still the best economic system. But must be reformed, in particular, their agents, the so called "political class", should be reformed. What we see is that the political class, in general, replaced the old monarchies and make every move in order to receive dividends. The corporate leaders do what they do because they are allowed by the political class. We shouldn't blame them by themselves. They are merely "traders". The big sinners are the political class... (I mean, in general, of course, but it is easy to spot who they are)."

Member 8: "I believe that the money system is just an illusion. Now money rules the world economics and politics. But we must wake up from the bad dream and reach to the true understanding of our world. Man cannot live by bread alone."

Member 9: "I believe it (capitalism) should be kept as it is."

Member 10: "Capitalism's turned us into competitive human beings (which I don't believe is good) and means we live in a system that benefits the rich and fucks the poor. Whether it's modified or replaced, I don't much care, as long as we can find a system that helps provide the necessities of life for everyone first. Then you can buy your Gucci dresses and blood diamonds."

Member 11: "Society must find a wise way to give

food, shelter, education and health care to everyone. The change from capitalism to another system, needs first a big change in the way the majority thinks."

Member 12: "Poverty could be solved instantly if we wanted it to be- which would reduce crime, benefit the economy and be better for all concerned (oh, other than that current 1% at the top, but they've had their turn). I think it's important we look beyond such things in the way that if someone says they're anti-capitalist it must mean they're a socialist, for instance. We base our understanding on the past and not with common sense in the present. Feed, house, give water and energy to everyone and the world would soon change for the better. THEN you can start trying to attain whatever else your heart desires. Capitalism, in its current form, certainly doesn't aid any of that."

Member 13: "Competition is the key to success. For rapid development, competition must be there."

Member 14: "I personally think there's a good and bad type of competition. Bad competition is where there's such scarcity or inequality that it becomes a dog-eat-dog world out of necessity. Good competition, or healthy competition, could happen in an environment where everyone has an opportunity to rise up and can at least get an education and healthcare and clean water and enough food. In that sort of environment, then competition can be a very good thing and competitors can all push each other to excel. However, I think unregulated Capitalism we have now is creating more often than not the dog-eat-dog-style competition..."

Member 15: "Our current system has gone into corporatism, collusion between government and industry, which is the primary problem IMHO. Lobbyists are running the government as opposed to the people. We need to get rid of career politicians and lobbyists, which would be the first step toward more equitable means. Co-ops tend to work well, likewise employee owned businesses which share the profit with their employees and investors. This helps get some of the profits to "normal" people but not what I would call socialism. Government bailouts are another thing that should end or be monitored more closely. If they do bail out a bank or corporation, it should be administered properly, not huge bonuses for the CEOs et al who drove the business into bankruptcy in the first place. CEOs should be paid a commission of sorts, based on the success of their leadership. If the company fails or loses money they should be fired, not rewarded. I don't have a problem with a leader being duly compensated for excellent ideas and leadership but when the company doesn't turn a profit then they should be ousted, not given a bonus."

Member 16: "Just reading Alain Touraine at the mo'. He suggests that there are currently two forms of capitalism running side-by-side at the moment. There is the actual productive capitalism - the people and factories that make stuff - and financial capitalism. The former is generally state-based (although there are, of course, trans-nationals) with real factories whereas the other is global and highly mobile - 'liquid' you might say, like Zigmunt Bauman. One serves society, one serves itself. At the moment, global financial capitalism is ascendant. But the 'real' economy is dependent in many ways on the state for sometimes covert support. Think of many of the widgets we all take for granted these days - GPS, the internet and the world wide web, even transistors all came out of government funded research. And an awful lot of this was the US government funding for defence. Think even today, we hear about face transplants funded in part by the US Navy. I suppose, really, it's just the military-industrial complex. But then the

116

whole thing is complicated by the need for energy - mainly electricity. And then you have the violent reactions to the post-colonialist politics in the middle-east and Africa. A command-capitalist economy like China starts to sound quite attractive. But to marry that with western Enlightenment individualism and a certain respect for human rights seems unlikely. Thus our governments start, in turn, to learn from those Silicon Valley Randians and start to harvest the data so freely provided by ourselves; in the end, we are the product. Doomed it is that we are!"

Member 17: "Surely the genius and greatest evil of capitalism is that we all become both product and customer, consumer and consumed?"

Member 18: "The problem is the scoundrels who live service to self. When good people do nothing, any good system can be used in negative ways. We are responsible for all negative use of Capitalism, which in itself is good. I see it is as the only choice for a free society. In fact, when we label a good system as the culprit on a topic, we make sure that the problem will not be corrected. We have to keep a clear head and THINK, not getting confused about systems, causes, effects, and corrections. Okay, Capitalism is not bad, but it is being used to the detriment of Earth and many people. We have to ask how to correct it. We must not talk about what "they" are doing as if we were helpless nothings. I may have said it before: Take responsibility. Take responsibility for your family and control of your own local neighborhood first, and outward to the (in our case) federal level. It's not by accident that we've been taught by the Controllers to look to the federal government for all answers. Capitalism and consumerism are two different things, as well. One does not imply the other. It is Us, the People, who decide to act like "good consumers". It is we who must change."

Member 19: "Capitalism by its nature relies on and encourages consumerism, but no, they're not the same thing. One is a concept and way of being, the other its tool. The problem is the urge exponential, driven by the shareholder system which demands not greater profits but greater increase in profits year-on-year. Merely making a profit is treated by the markets as a loss..."

Member 20: "The problem is not capitalism. The problem is in ourselves. As it is often said that we all have God (or Gods) inside our being, we all also have Lucifer, the one that wants science, commerce, Exchange, trade, bridges, airplanes and a lot of pollution...If we are not in enough number (critical mass) with knowledge, awareness and wisdom, humanity will always be well below its fantastic potential. After the fall of the fascist regime in Portugal, I witness the communist upheaval here and in Africa with the same mental frame as the fascist executioners. The fall of the Soviet Union have shown that humans are not yet ready for a big change. Those that want to push for a change without a massive human awareness, are preparing the way to live in caves."

Member 21: "I believe that the agents (the politicians) that should guarantee the democratic functioning of the State, are doing exactly the opposite (in this sense Max Weber was wrong in his analysis). The reform should start with their statute in society and they must be subject to citizen control like Iceland did recently (and they are back to normality faster than any other country, according to the IMF...)"

Member 22: "Capitalism did not cause the Global Cabal and its Illuminati to take over in the USA. Rather, it was that the people slept through their watch over government, especially locally. The Cabal took over medicine with their paradigm of germs and drug or cut, and promotion of their Big Pharma. Does that mean that medicine is bad? They took over our local schools, universities (to a large extent), and media, after stating that they would dumb us down. Does that mean that media and our former system of local control of schools is bad? No, on all counts. They took over taxing, banking, credit, financing and financials, treasury and currency, while we took no mind, turning it into a system of enslavement, so that when you get paid it almost all goes to them. And for them it was never about money, but their power and our personal energy. How can you restructure a system that, if not taken over by thieves and controllers, has no structure? When we have the freedom to walk down the street, but someone comes up and mugs us, is the answer to take away our freedom to walk down the street? No. So arrest the muggers. Similarly, don't throw out the freedom of capitalism. It is not free market capitalism, but the fraudulent, controlling, banksters' systems (including their Illuminati faux government that is not the USA and extends into the states and cities) that need to be eliminated. THEY are systematically, purposely causing the problems that are blamed on capitalism. But they are on the way out, as you will see when you focus off their mass media and look around. So let their systems continue to crumble, while finding new, loving and out of the box solutions, starting locally. I'm looking to the children of you young guys to give us the solutions. Those kids are different. They will not be controlled."

Member 23: "When you speak of "them", I read "the political class"... In my point of view, they are the ones to blame. They took power like a "new" social class that intermarry their children from the "left" to the "right" wings to guarantee their dynasty. They occupied the void created with the retirement from power of the old monarchies. They live with the over taxation imposed by force to those

119

that work hard and contribute with creative thinking and action to the benefit of our society. I believe that, one day, the politicians will be confronted worldwide with this central issue. Politics should be a service to our societies, not a means to live."

Member 24: "I don't think what's needed is a knee-jerk reaction or to throw the baby (capitalism) out with the bathwater. Instead, society needs to recognize that the current free market system ain't doing what it is supposed to and that capitalism in the 21st century isn't yielding the same returns for the common man as it did in the mid-late 20th century. I believe with homeless numbers increasing, not to mention unemployment, that capitalism (and perhaps the entire financial system) needs to be restructured ASAP."

Member 25: "Capitalism has its advantages, motivation to better oneself being an important one. I'm not convinced however, that we cannot have compassion and ambition in the same form of government. Compassion in the form of basic needs being met first. Everyone gets a piece of the pie, after that, go ahead and fight for a bigger piece of the pie, if of what is left after the basics are met."

The final result of our Underground Knowledge group poll was as follows:

-53.7% of members voted capitalism should be *restructured/reformed*

-26.9% of members voted capitalism should be *replaced by another economic system*

-10.4% of members voted *unsure*

-9% voted capitalism should be *left exactly as is*

So, more than half the members believe capitalism should be restructured/reformed.

We believe this poll result is reasonably reflective of the public at large. People are sick of being screwed by banksters and by corrupt politicians who do nothing to stop them. However, most people seem to want to keep the best aspects of our current (capitalistic) society.

The poll result is also reflective of our own opinion in that we think restructuring or reforming the current version of capitalism is what's most needed.

It's time for change. Let's face it, a resentful public are perhaps only one or two major financial injustices away from demanding a new, fairer economic system that supports 'the people' ahead of the global elite.

15

Restructuring Capitalism

"The powers of financial capitalism had another far reaching aim, nothing less than to create a world system of financial control in private hands able to dominate the political system of each country and the economy of the world as a whole." –Prof. Caroll Quigley, Georgetown University, *Tragedy and Hope* (1966)

C learly, many of the issues in this book are related to capitalism. With its profits-over-people agenda, capitalism has unfortunately spawned a monster that's now out of control.

The free enterprise concept inherent in the economic model of capitalism should mean common people, or lower and middle class wage-earners, have greater potential to rise up and gain financial independence. In reality, however, free enterprise all too often leads to an almost total lack of government regulation that in turn allows the global elite to run amuck in Gordon Gecko-style financial coups.

Even if capitalism is the best economic system in theory – which it probably is – the type of corporatocracy it leads to in the real world usually means the rich get richer while the poor get poorer. And though much good has come from capitalism – America's phenomenal success in the 20th Century was arguably due to the free market economics its Founding Father's encouraged – the system's immense flaws have also become evident in recent years.

It's almost as if capitalism is a robot that was originally programmed with a single instruction: *Make profits by all means necessary.*

Initially the profits surged in, putting food on the table for untold families, building communities and lifting living standards in numerous countries. However, the robot could not be stopped or reprogrammed, and without governments being able, or willing, to set boundaries the same system that once *gave* to the people now began to *take* from them. It began to lower living standards by widening the gap between rich and poor and by destroying the same communities it once built.

Unregulated capitalism began to abuse working class citizens – the very people it was designed to assist; it allowed leaders of corporations to play God while employees became workhorses for their owners. Perhaps a better description would be worker bees sacrificing their own welfare for the benefit of the royal queen bees.

Unfortunately, the advanced civilization and technological utopia that capitalism helped create is also one where most humans are treated like dogs in a dog-eat-dog world.

"Economic fundamentalists do not care what happens to society or western civilisation or the world at large, or even their own work-mates, or their own shareholders, just so long as they get, as payout, enough to live on in prosperous comfort for the rest of their lives." –Bob Ellis, *The Capitalism Delusion*

Above: *A quote on display by Martin Luther King, Jr.*
"'Today capitalism has outlived its usefulness' MLK"
by Liz Mc - Flickr:
'Today capitalism has outlived its usefulness' MLK.
Licensed under CC BY 2.0 via Wikimedia Commons

None of this means we are socialists or communists. Nor are we anti-progress. And no, we are not about to suddenly reveal that this whole book has been a thinly veiled disguise for our political beliefs.

For those who have read this book in its entirety, and indeed the rest of *The Underground Knowledge Series*, it should be abundantly clear we are staunchly apolitical and believe that no political system can ever provide a total solution.

Most of the issues we've raised in this book are actually social concerns rather than economic or political ones.

Also, as filmmakers and authors, we are fully aware that we have benefited, and continue to benefit, from a capitalistic system. There is surely much good in capitalism. For example, *the American Dream* – the same dream that people of most other nations desire – says anyone who has ambition and a good work ethic can succeed no matter their race, gender or social class.

Living up to those ideals is likely possible only in a free, democratic *and* capitalistic society.

Therefore, we would support a revised form of capitalism, rather than doing away with it completely. This restructured economic system would, hopefully, be one with more heart and social awareness while still allowing for self-made entrepreneurs to rise up and be rewarded for their efforts. Rewarding achievers is crucial as history has proven that whenever socialism or communism is implemented there's little incentive to succeed because success is not duly rewarded.

It's obvious something has to change in our capitalistic society as there's far too much unnecessary suffering on the planet right now.

Connecting the Dots

What do all the quotes, articles, facts, opinions, rumors, economic theories and mere conjecture throughout this book mean regarding banking and the monetary system?

Admittedly, many of the points raised simply lead to more questions.

Questions such as:

Is the Federal Reserve designed to be the biggest money laundering institution in the world?

Are there really powerful groups operating behind the scenes, manipulating governments, economies and the financial markets with effortless ease? If so, how are they able to hide their deceitful activities?

Do journalists purposefully obscure the truths surrounding the Fed in order not to upset the powers that be? Or is the average journalist simply unaware of the shady history of the Fed?

Who are the Financial Overlords manipulating the markets in their favor? Are they the elite banking families, the likes of the Vatican Bank, or other more shadowy figures?

We do not have any definitive answers to such questions, but all we know is there *has got to be* a fairer financial system that protects the world's poor and working classes.

126

So, perhaps the most important question of all is:

How many more individuals, communities and countries have to go bankrupt before the big changes we all anxiously await are finally devised and implemented?

Maybe advances in the Internet and new cyber technologies might be part of this long-awaited change. We do wonder how cybermoney, or cryptocurrencies, will influence the world economy, and whether this 21st Century phenomenon might provide a means for the common people to circumvent the all-pervasive web of central banking.

Did you know, the world's most popular form of cybermoney is Bitcoin? *The Age of Cryptocurrency: How Bitcoin and Digital Money Are Challenging the Global Economic Order*, by Paul Vigna and Michael J. Casey, is one of the best books on the Bitcoin phenomenon.

The book's synopsis informs us as follows:

"Bitcoin became a buzzword overnight. A cyber-enigma with an enthusiastic following, it pops up in headlines and fuels endless media debate. You can apparently use it to buy anything from coffee to cars, yet few people seem to truly understand what it is. This raises the question: Why should anyone care about bitcoin?

"In The Age of Cryptocurrency, Wall Street journalists Paul Vigna and Michael J. Casey deliver the definitive answer to this question. Cybermoney is poised to launch a revolution, one that could reinvent traditional financial and social structures while bringing the world's billions of "unbanked" individuals into a new global economy. Cryptocurrency holds the promise of a financial system without a middleman, one owned by the people who use it and one safeguarded from the devastation of a 2008-

type crash.

"It implies, above all, monumental and wide-reaching change-for better and for worse. But it is here to stay, and you ignore it at your peril".

The Age of Cryptocurrency synopsis also points out that the "digital currency world will look very different from the paper currency world".

We can only hope that all future economic development, whether brought about by new technologies or otherwise, places more monies into the hands of the average citizen, not to mention curtails the powers of international banksters!

Finally, for the ultimate solution to all the financial problems we've outlined, perhaps what's needed is not so much a *redistribution of wealth*, which sounds a bit communistic to our liking, but rather a *reclaiming of stolen monies* – monies stolen by the global banking elite; monies that rightfully below to *we, the people, the majority, the 99%.*

THE END

If you liked this book, the authors would greatly appreciate a review from you on Amazon.

And if you wish to discuss the material in this book, or other interrelated alternative topics, we invite you to join our Underground Knowledge global discussion group on Goodreads.

For your reading pleasure, an excerpt from *Genius Intelligence*, book one in The Underground Knowledge Series, follows...

GENIUS INTELLIGENCE:

Secret Techniques and Technologies to Increase IQ

James & Lance

MORCAN

Table of Contents

Foreword

This book is part of *The Underground Knowledge Series*, written by James & Lance Morcan, authors of a much needed, perceptive summary of the darker aspects of world reality titled *The Orphan Conspiracies*, which I also wrote a foreword for.

I was employed for many years as a senior research scientist developing naval underwater weapon systems at the Technical Research and Development Institute of the Ministry of Defense, Japan. During this period, I spent a lot of time in my private life studying *Number Theory*, which is a branch of pure mathematics devoted primarily to the study of the integers, or whole numbers.

From this mathematical research, I came across the enigma of Srinivasa Ramanujan, an Indian genius mathematician who, with almost no formal training, discovered many complex formulas and made extraordinary contributions to mathematical analysis and number theory. Ramanujan often said the Goddess of Namakkal inspired him with formulae at night while he was dreaming and that each morning, upon awakening, he would write down the results of these vivid dreams.

For many years, I could not understand the mental processes that lead to Ramanujan's advanced mathematical findings. However, after studying the human brain from the standpoint of superluminal particles, I eventually came to the conclusion that everyone's brain has the potential to connect to an outer field of consciousness, which has also been termed by more mystical thinkers as the Universal Mind.

Above: Srinivasa Ramanujan
"Srinivasa Ramanujan - OPC - 1" by Konrad Jacobs
Oberwolfach Photo Collection, original location.
Licensed under CC-BY-SA-2.0-de via Wikimedia Commons

To summarize my research on the brain, I wrote *Superluminal Particles and Hypercomputation*, which was published by LAMBERT Academic Publishing in early 2014. Soon after its publication, I was contacted by James Morcan, one of the authors of *Genius Intelligence*, who felt that my theories on superluminal particles could support his and Lance Morcan's suppositions about the nature of genius.

This book you are now reading contains a wide range of genius methods – all of which have the potential to increase your IQ. You'll read about everything from speed reading to brain gland activation to sleep learning to smart drugs to virtual reality training.

I believe this is a much needed book for those who sense there are faster and easier ways to learn and study than the methods currently being taught in mainstream education systems.

Lastly, I sincerely hope that the publication of *Genius Intelligence* contributes to a global awakening to assist us to hold enough truth in our minds to change this world for better.

Dr. Takaaki Musha

Director of the Advanced-Science Technology Research Organization, Yokohama, Japan.

Former senior research scientist at the Technical Research and Development Institute of the Ministry of Defense, Japan.

Introduction

The genesis for this book was fiction rather than reality.

Now we've revealed that, you would be forgiven for assuming none of what follows on the mightily complex subject of intelligence and increasing IQ is true.

Before we attempt to put your mind at ease on that score, we have a few more revelations to get out of the way…

Neither of us has any formal education qualifications of note, having barely completed high school. Nor has either of us ever taken an IQ test and therefore it cannot be proven we have high intelligence just as it cannot be disproven we are complete idiots!

About now, you'd also be forgiven for asking why we, of all people, have written a book on intelligence and the nature of genius.

On the fiction versus reality issue, it's not quite as alarming as it sounds, we hope.

You see, the fictional reference actually relates to our international thriller series of novels titled *The Orphan Trilogy*.

The decision to write this thriller series was made a decade ago, and it marks the commencement of our journey. A journey to discover what makes a genius and, more importantly, what makes a genius tick.

In *The Ninth Orphan*, book one in the trilogy, our mysterious lead character (who is known only as Nine) is not only an assassin, but also a mental genius who exhibits a level of intelligence rarely if ever seen in any character in literature. Nine has a photographic memory, can read entire books in five minutes flat and speaks dozens of languages. Plus he learns new skills extremely fast and is highly adaptable – so much so he's nicknamed *the human chameleon*.

How Nine reached that level of intelligence, though, is merely implied or hinted at in the first book in the series.

In its prequel, *The Orphan Factory*, we had to design an education system that would reveal exactly how Nine and his fellow orphans grew up to become that smart. This was quite a challenge as our setting was no Ivy League college. Rather, it was the Pedemont Orphanage, a rundown institution in Riverdale, one of Chicago's poorest neighborhoods.

Having both gone through the traditional education system and finding it laborious and uninspiring, we quickly discovered it was fun to brainstorm alternative and more advanced forms of study for our trilogy. Even so, it took many years of investigating accelerated learning methods – some rare, some not so rare – before we felt confident enough to write about what it would take to create youngsters with intellects as advanced as those of our Pedemont orphans.

All the insights unearthed during that 10-year investigative period (spent examining the great historical minds and studying little-known intelligence boosting methods) are revealed in *Genius Intelligence*.

Highlights of our exploration into the world of super learning include many fascinating discoveries, which were totally new – to us at least and, we expect, in most cases will be new to you, too – and which were certainly outside our personal experience collectively and individually.

Those discoveries include:

- Individuals (living and dead) with IQ's far higher than Einstein's.
- Brain waves common to geniuses – and the various ways to induce those brain waves.
- Mental techniques the world's elite and A-List celebrities are quietly using to help them process information while they're asleep or in *virtual* worlds.
- Chemical substances students and academics the world over employ to kick-start the brain into overdrive.
- Cutting-edge technologies business tycoons and professional athletes employ to achieve a mental edge on their competitors.

Beyond these random examples, one of the key discoveries we made is that every human brain has enormous potential – possibly even *unlimited* potential.

No matter the challenging circumstances – whether ADHD, dyslexia or mental illness – it makes no difference when it comes to the brain's *latent* potential. The capacity for achieving genius levels of intelligence remains the same. After all, there has been many a genius with learning disabilities, hyperactivity and genetic brain disorders.

The latest scientific studies have revealed extraordinary findings. The brain is much more flexible and adaptable than previously thought. It can evolve and creatively work around limitations and nullify them.

Examples of this phenomenon even include brain-damaged individuals who have been shown to be capable of achieving equal intelligence to the average person.

How or why this is possible is because of the brain's incredible capacity to restructure itself.

This rewiring process falls under a category in neuroscience known as *neuroplasticity* – a broad term used to describe the brain's ability to form new neural connections or to reorganize itself in an attempt to overcome or diminish the effects of old age, substance abuse or traumatic head injury.

Neuroplasticity is scientific proof that intelligence is *not* something that is locked by a certain age or that cannot fluctuate or increase.

Not receiving a college degree or even a high school education doesn't mean genius abilities are out of the question. The same applies for those who come from a background of extreme poverty.

History is littered with examples of uneducated and semi-educated individuals from impoverished backgrounds who have gone on to educate themselves and deliver revolutionary breakthroughs within academic circles, the corporate world, the arts and other walks of life.

When the brain's potential is fully unleashed, there can be few if any limitations. Anyone who tells you otherwise isn't up-to-date with the latest scientific findings on the brain and is exhibiting their ignorance. For the brain's potential *is* the human potential…

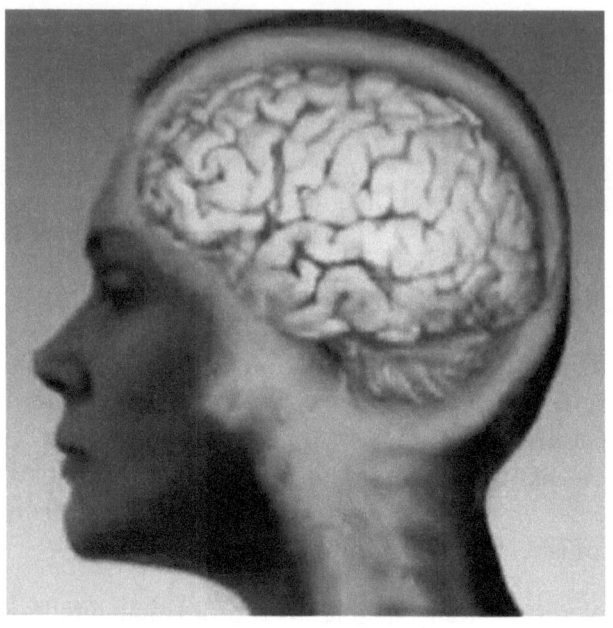

Above: The brain…unlimited potential?
"Human brain female side view" by National Institute of Health
Licensed under Public Domain via Wikimedia Commons

The other crucial discovery – perhaps *the* most crucial – to come out of our research is that higher intelligence is not necessarily something you're born with or genetically predisposed toward. In fact, most instances of above-the-ordinary intelligences are usually *acquired* thru superior learning techniques – many of which we cover in detail in this book.

Reading about the greatest minds in history, including recent history, more often than not reveals the individuals concerned (or people close to them) employed specific learning methods. The examples we cite throughout this book shatter the myth that geniuses are always born with exceptional intelligence and/or talent.

Certainly, there are those born with amazing abilities not fostered by educational methods, but our research has revealed these naturally gifted geniuses are definitely the exception, not the norm.

A classic example of this natural born genius myth is Wolfgang Amadeus Mozart whom most believe was simply a wunderkind, or virtuoso, from infancy. Many brain researchers have also described the Austrian composer as someone who just had incredible musical and artistic abilities from birth.

Above: Mozart as a child
"Wolfgang-amadeus-mozart 2" by Anonymous
possibly by Pietro Antonio Lorenzoni (1721-1782)
Portrait owned by the Mozarteum, Salzburg.
Licensed under Public Domain via Wikimedia Commons

However, as with most geniuses, there is a significant body of evidence to support the contentious theory that

Mozart's brilliance was as much the result of *nurture* as it was *nature*, if not more so.

It is true the musical prodigy was composing by five, and by seven or so he was performing for audiences throughout Europe. And while achievements like that, at those early ages, are certainly extraordinary, the key point is that Mozart came from a musical family and was pushed to excel musically. As soon as he could walk and talk, in fact, or even earlier if you stop to consider he was exposed to classical compositions while still in his mother's womb.

The young Mozart's father Leopold was a renowned composer in his own right and an ambitious musical teacher who wanted his son to achieve greatness. History tells us that Leopold forced Mozart Junior to practice for many hours a day even before he had reached school age.

It has been estimated that by the time Mozart was six he had already spent about 4000 hours studying music.

Perhaps a modern-day equivalent to Mozart's father would be someone like Richard Williams, father of legendary American tennis champions Serena and Venus Williams. Upon deciding tennis was the way out of the 'ghetto', Williams Sr. pushed his daughters day after day from a young age in his relentless quest for them to become world champions.

Classical music experts have noted that many of Mozart's childhood compositions are mostly rearrangements of other (older) composers' works. Not being experts in classical music – or any music for that matter – we can't comment, but if true that would further undermine the enduring myth about the great composer being an innate genius who could rely solely on his natural talent and who hardly needed to practice.

142

We found that nine out of ten biographies of geniuses reveal forgotten or previously unmentioned examples of intelligence-enhancing techniques and/or technologies these individuals employed on their path to greatness.

Traditionally, IQ has been perceived as a genetic trait in much the same way an individual's height or body type is perceived – in other words a fixed trait, or state, and therefore (thought to be) something that could never be altered.

In recent years, however, there has been an explosion of new scientific studies, which make a mockery of that assumption. These show that cognitive training, whether by mental techniques or brain enhancement technologies, can definitely deliver intelligence-boosting effects.

Certainly, you need some natural aptitude to excel in most facets of life – be it mental, physical or artistic – but if genius was simply a matter of inheriting good genes, then many more of us would be geniuses.

Anyway, we predict, or sincerely hope, that formal education will one day be reflective of what occurs within the fictional Pedemont Orphanage of our thriller series – minus the assassination training of course!

Equally, we firmly believe some if not most of the alternative learning methods mentioned in *Genius Intelligence* will eventually become the norm for students the world over.

To return to that other awkward subject – who we are and what the hell we are doing writing about the secrets of the genius mindset. Well, that's a trickier one to satisfy readers on so early in the piece…

All we can really say is we write fiction and non-fiction books and produce movies in our dual careers as authors and filmmakers. In our earlier careers, we have between us held a variety of positions in different fields spanning the arts, media, PR and retail sectors. Those positions include journalist, bookseller, publicist and newspaper editor.

So we shall have to leave it up to you as to whether you think this book is a work of "genius" or not.

One reason we wrote this book is because, in our opinion, most other titles on the subject of increasing intelligence make for disappointing reading. In the main, they are not written for the average person. They're written *for* academics *by* people with PhD's.

The end result, more often than not, are books that resemble academic text and which rarely venture beyond scientifically proven and well-established mainstream methodologies.

Paradoxical though it may sound, we are convinced that *not* being from the world of academia, or even being particularly studious, eminently qualified us to write this book. After all, we wrote it to empower the average individual – the 'common' working class person. We can relate to such people as that's exactly our background.

One thing we can promise is that after researching far and wide in some unusual and unlikely places, the pages of this book contain the most advanced accelerated learning methods available on the planet.

Wishing you well on your path to increasing your IQ!

James & Lance MORCAN

1

Genius Techniques of the Elite

I t has long been speculated that secret societies, mystery schools, intelligence agencies and other clandestine organizations have advanced learning methods superior to anything taught in even the most prestigious universities. Methods which are only ever taught to the chosen few – initiates who have all sworn an oath to keep the group's syllabus *in house* and never reveal any of the teachings to outsiders.

On the rare occasions the public get wind of these types of advanced learning techniques – usually via information leaked to the Internet, sometimes via published books – they are seldom tested or given the attention they deserve and so largely remain in obscurity. One reason for this could be the advanced techniques are often not comprehensible because whoever is behind them has withheld the overall curriculum.

There's many a tale of mysterious figures from secretive groups mastering skills, languages and even complex career paths so quickly that most would say it's impossible.

But that opinion assumes we common people know of, or have access to, all the learning methods known to man.

If we are to assume there are superior learning methods not taught in our mainstream education system then this naturally leads to other questions.

What if your child's top-notch education is actually a second-rate education?

Or, if you are a student, what if that professor you look up to is no mastermind, but just a tool of an inferior learning institution?

None of this is to disrespect formal education. It plays a vital role in society and the betterment of Mankind, and only a fool would doubt the importance of getting a good education.

Nor are we suggesting there isn't the odd learning institution that teaches at least some accelerated learning techniques, although such establishments would probably exist on the fringes of mainstream education.

The Montessori system is possibly one such example as it allows children to have greater freedom of expression and to learn in playful and organic ways.

Successful alumni of the Montessori education system include Amazon founder Jeff Bezos, Nobel Prize-winning author Gabriel García Márquez, Wikipedia founder Jimmy Wales, tennis champion Roger Federer and Google co-founders Sergey Brin and Larry Page.

Above: Roger Federer...Montessori alumni
"R Federer Australian Open 2014" by Peter Myers from Melbourne, Australia
Federer - Oz Open 2014. Licensed under CC BY 2.0 via Wikimedia Commons

In general, however, accelerated learning methods are more likely to be found outside the modern education system.

Let's face it, wherever in the world you go, real prodigies are the exception not the norm in the present system. Those rare individuals whom society labels as geniuses are almost always *freaks of nature* and are *naturally gifted* rather than being diligent students who became geniuses as a result of their education.

"I'll be a genius and the world will admire me. Perhaps I'll be despised and misunderstood, but I'll be a genius, a great genius." – Salvador Dalí. Written in his diary at the age of 16.

2

Polymaths and High-IQ Individuals

"The purpose of having the orphans study all these diverse fields was not for them to just become geniuses, but to become polymaths – meaning they would be geniuses in a wide variety of fields. Whether they were studying the sciences, languages, international finance, politics, the arts or martial arts, they would not stop until they'd achieved complete mastery of that subject. Kentbridge himself had encyclopedic knowledge about almost everything, and expected nothing less from his orphans." –The Ninth Orphan.

A book critic who reviewed *The Ninth Orphan*, book one in our thriller series, criticized our protagonist Nine (the ninth-born orphan) for having an IQ, or intelligence quotient, higher than Einstein's. The strong implication in the review was that this was a ridiculous character decision we, the authors, had made.

That all sounds like a valid criticism on the surface, but had this critic gone beyond his own sphere of knowledge and done a little research he would have discovered there are many people whose IQ's have been recorded to be higher than Einstein's.

American author Marilyn Vos Savant, for example, has an IQ of 192; Russian chess grandmaster and former world champion Garry Kasparov has an IQ of 194. Incidentally, Einstein's IQ was estimated in the 1920's to between 160 and 190.

But wait, there's much more when it comes to the world of super geniuses…

Quite a few individuals have tested in excess of a 200 IQ score, including South Korean civil engineer Kim Ung-yong (210), former child prodigy and NASA employee Christopher Hirata (225) and Australian mathematician Terence Tao (225-230).

And last but not least is American child prodigy, mathematician and politician William James Sidis who had an IQ of 250-300. He graduated grammar school at age six, went to Harvard University at age 11 and graduated *cum laude* at the age of 16. Sidis, who died in 1944, could fluently speak 40 languages by the time he reached adulthood.

Above: Sidis…20th Century child prodigy.
"William James Sidis 1914" by Unknown - The Sidis Archives.
Licensed under Public Domain via Wikimedia Commons

Remember, the average IQ is 100 and approximately 50% of those tested score between 90 and 110.

According to the book *IQ and the Wealth of Nations*, by Dr. Richard Lynn and Dr. Tatu Vanhanen, the top five countries in terms of average IQ's of their citizens are Hong Kong (107), South Korea (106), Japan (105), Taiwan (104) and Singapore (103). Further down the list, China, New Zealand and the UK share equal 12th position with a 100 average, while the US is in 19th position with an average citizen IQ of 98.

However, many scholars in the 21st Century now believe IQ scores aren't everything and it's likely areas of intelligence exist that cannot be measured in any test. This is possibly substantiated by the number of successful and iconic individuals who recorded very low IQ scores. These include the once highly articulate and outspoken boxer Muhammad Ali who, as a young man, scored only 78 – an IQ so low it supposedly denotes a mild mental disability!

And of course, the list of the world's so-called most intelligent *excludes* extremely bright individuals in impoverished parts of the world where IQ's are, or were, rarely tested. The Indian mathematical genius, Srinivasa Ramanujan (1887-1920), was an example of such incredible geniuses who defy all explanation.

You'll recall Dr. Takaaki Musha refers to Ramanujan in the Foreword, mentioning how he was inspired by the gentleman's advanced mathematical findings.

Born into poverty in Erode, India, Ramanujan discovered extraordinary mathematical formulas despite being self-taught with no formal training in mathematics. He changed the face of mathematics as we know it and left many highly-educated and acclaimed Western mathematicians completely gobsmacked.

Furthermore, the other high-IQ individuals mentioned earlier are only in the top bracket of those who *agreed* to undergo IQ tests *and* allow their scores to be published.

It's quite conceivable certain elite individuals belonging to secret societies, mystery schools or intelligence agencies do not reveal their IQ scores. That secret intelligence factor was the basis for our fictional Pedemont orphans in *The Orphan Trilogy* whom we either state or imply have IQ's of around 200 or higher.

As a result of the accelerated learning techniques within the diverse curriculum that begins before they can even walk or talk, the orphans can assimilate and retain phenomenal amounts of information. By their teens, the child prodigies are more knowledgeable even than adult geniuses. They can solve complex problems, are fully knowledgeable about almost any current world subject or historical event, and are to all intents and purposes organic supercomputers and human library databases.

Our orphans are exposed to highly advanced learning methods so that they will have at their disposal all the necessary skills and information to be able to overcome life-and-death problems that may arise on future espionage assignments. They're taught there is no challenge or question that cannot be overcome, solved or answered as long as they fully utilize the power of their minds.

Each child at the Pedemont Orphanage eventually becomes a *polymath* – a person who is beyond a genius. It's a word we use throughout the trilogy as we felt it best describes the orphans' off-the-scale intellects.

A polymath is actually a *multiple-subject genius*. However, the criterion for a polymath is someone who is an expert in vastly different, almost unrelated fields. For example, an artist who works in the film, theatre and literary industries and who is a masterful actor, screenwriter, novelist, film director and film producer would *not* qualify as a polymath as those fields are all artistic mediums and closely related.

Rather, a polymath is someone who has excelled in, or completely mastered, a variety of unrelated or loosely related subjects. These could be as diverse as economics, dance, architecture, mathematics, history, forensic science, cooking and entomology.

And before you go calling yourself a polymath, don't forget you must be an *expert* in each field. Unfortunately, being a jack-of-all-trades and master-of-none doesn't count.

One of the best examples of a polymath is Leonardo da Vinci.

Born in Italy in 1452, Leonardo was a sculptor, painter, architect, mathematician, musician, engineer, inventor, anatomist, botanist, geologist, cartographer and writer. Although he received an informal education that included geometry, Latin and mathematics, he was essentially an *autodidact*, or a self-taught individual.

Above: Portrait of Leonardo da Vinci c. 1510
"Francesco Melzi - Portrait of Leonardo - WGA14795" by Francesco Melzi
Web Gallery of Art. Licensed under Public Domain via Wikimedia Commons

The man who many have called *the* most diversely talented person who ever lived, left behind an array of masterpieces in the painting world alone, including *The Last Supper*, *Mona Lisa* and *The Vitruvian Man*.

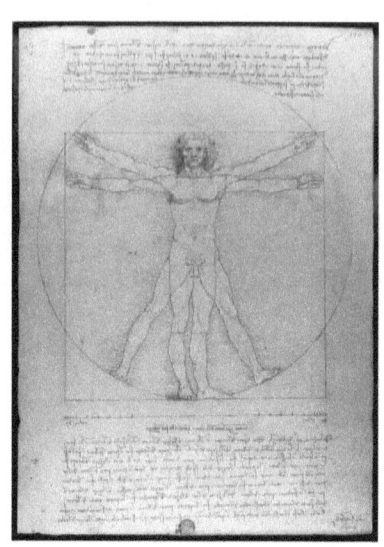

"The knowledge of all things is possible" –Leonardo da Vinci

3

Outrunning the Conscious Mind

"The subconscious was always favored over the everyday conscious mind, which was considered too slow to be effective." –The Orphan Factory

Developing a genius mindset essentially comes down to two things: operating at speed and using the subconscious mind more than the conscious. This intuitive or relaxed approach to study is the polar opposite of traditional and mainstream forms of education.

Apart from some artistic subjects like music or dance, learning institutions generally require pupils to concentrate hard at all times. In other words, students have no choice but to always use their conscious minds, thereby suppressing the great reservoir of the subconscious.

When we are forced to think s-l-o-w-l-y like this our brain functions at well below optimum levels. That's why school students often feel exhausted as studying in this fashion is incredibly draining.

But how can we feel mentally drained when neuroscientists and brain researchers agree we each only use a tiny percentage of our brain?

155

In *The Orphan Trilogy*, our orphans often go into a daydream state whenever they need answers to life-and-death situations. This is because when you defocus you allow your intuitive self, or your subconscious mind, to *deliver* the answers you need. It just happens, without reaching for it.

We've all experienced pondering a problem all day long only to find we *receive* the solution when forgetting about the problem and thinking of something else. When we stop concentrating so hard, we allow our subconscious to flourish, and those who do this more than others are sometimes called geniuses.

As head of the Pedemont Orphanage, Tommy Kentbridge says to his students in *The Orphan Factory*, "The subconscious mind is where all higher intelligences exist. Every genius throughout history – Tesla, Einstein, Da Vinci – tapped into the infinite power of their subconscious minds."

Studies have shown the subconscious mind can process around 11 million bits of information per second. The conscious mind, however, can only process about 15 to 16 bits of information per second.

Quite a difference!

One of the best ways to bring the subconscious mind into the equation is to *outrun* the conscious mind by going so fast it literally can't keep up. So, at Chicago's Pedemont Orphanage, our orphans do everything at speed. They're also taught how to learn things indirectly instead of directly. By skirting around the edges of complex subjects, the children never get information overload or lose their way.

As we wrote in *The Ninth Orphan*, "In the tradition of Leonardo da Vinci and history's other great polymaths, the children were taught how to fully understand anything by using an advanced mental technique where they would simply *life* their minds into comprehension."

To life your mind into comprehension is once again the polar opposite of modern education systems which imply there's only one way to learn: consciously and with intense concentration.

While this indirect way of learning may sound flaky, it is actually backed up by hard science and is not remotely mystical. This approach is about brainwaves and understanding, or recognizing, the optimal state for learning.

When you hit the right groove, it's possible to learn quickly and in a satisfying, even enjoyable, fashion.

It is that singularity of mind top sportsmen and martial arts masters achieve. Psychologists sometimes refer to this ultimate mental state as *the zone*, but it's really just about having the most effective brainwaves for learning.

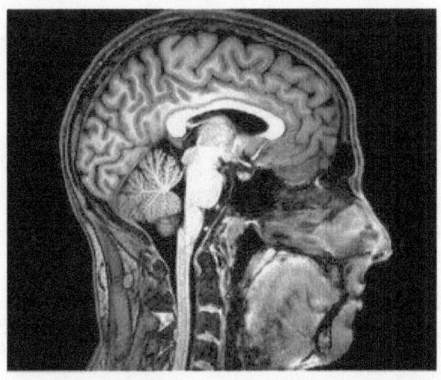

Above: A high quality T3 fMRI brain scan
"FMRI Brain Scan" by DrOONeil - Own work.
Licensed under CC BY-SA 3.0 via Wikimedia Commons

Any time study feels laborious the student is most likely in the beta brainwave, which occurs when the conscious mind is governing. A beta-dominant mind is the perfect recipe for mediocrity and boredom.

The subconscious mind comes into play in other less common brainwaves such as alpha, gamma, theta and delta. These brainwaves have also been shown to be activated when test subjects are laughing, daydreaming, meditating, singing, dancing or spontaneously moving about.

Now how many math or English teachers would tolerate those activities in their classrooms?

What if there really is a much quicker, less methodical way of learning that allows you to learn without learning?

Sounds paradoxical, doesn't it?

"Talent hits a target no one else can hit. Genius hits a target no one else can see." –Arthur Schopenhauer

Other books by Lance & James Morcan follow over page...

Other books by Lance & James Morcan published by Sterling Gate Books

HISTORICAL FICTION:

White Spirit (A novel based on a true story)
Into the Americas (A novel based on a true story)
World Odyssey (The World Duology, #1)
Fiji: A Novel (The World Duology, #2)

CONSPIRACY THRILLERS:

The Ninth Orphan (The Orphan Trilogy, #1)
The Orphan Factory (The Orphan Trilogy, #2)
The Orphan Uprising (The Orphan Trilogy, #3)

CRIME THRILLERS:

Silent Fear (A novel inspired by true crimes)
The Me Too Girl
The Heathrow Affair

ACTION-ADVENTURE:

High Country Contract
The Dogon Initiative (The Deniables, Book 1)

SHORT STORY BOX SET BY LANCE MORCAN

5 SHORT STORY GEMS: Once Were Brothers / Mr. 100% / A Gladiator's Love / The Last Tasmanian Tiger / Brooklyn Bankster

NON-FICTION:

DEBUNKING HOLOCAUST DENIAL THEORIES: Two Non-Jews Affirm the Historicity of the Nazi Genocide

THE ORPHAN CONSPIRACIES: 29 Conspiracy Theories from The Orphan Trilogy

GENIUS INTELLIGENCE: Secret Techniques and Technologies to Increase IQ (The Underground Knowledge Series, #1)

ANTIGRAVITY PROPULSION: Human or Alien Technologies? (The Underground Knowledge Series, #2)

MEDICAL INDUSTRIAL COMPLEX: The $ickness Industry, Big Pharma and Suppressed Cures (The Underground Knowledge Series, #3)

THE CATCHER IN THE RYE ENIGMA: J.D. Salinger's Mind Control Triggering Device or a Coincidental Literary Obsession of Criminals? (The Underground Knowledge Series, #4)

INTERNATIONAL BANKSTER$: The Global Banking Elite Exposed and the Case for Restructuring Capitalism (The Underground Knowledge Series, #5)

BANKRUPTING THE THIRD WORLD: How the Global Elite Drown Poor Nations in a Sea of Debt (The Underground Knowledge Series, #6)

UNDERGROUND BASES: Subterranean Military Facilities and the Cities Beneath Our Feet (The Underground Knowledge Series, #7)

VACCINE SCIENCE REVISITED: Are Childhood Immunizations As Safe As Claimed? (The Underground Knowledge Series, #8)